Elephants on the Rampage

Elephants on the Rampage

The Eclipse of American Conservatism

Sara Jarman
with Brent Gilchrist, Ph.D.

Copyright © 2017 by Sara Jarman with Brent Gilchrist, Ph.D.
All rights reserved. No part of this publication may be reproduced, distributed, or transmitted in any form or by any means, including photocopying, recording, or other electronic or mechanical methods, without the prior written permission of the publisher, except in the case of brief quotations embodied in critical reviews and certain other noncommercial uses permitted by copyright law.

ISBN: 1540362337
ISBN 13: 9781540362339

For Heather Jarman

In Memory of Brent Gilchrist

Table of Contents

	A Note to the Reader ix
	Introduction Authentic Conservatism, Movement Conservatism and the Republican Party xiii
One	Conservatism as an Ideology 1
Two	The End of History and the Death of Politics 16
Three	"The Reagan Revolution" 28
Four	The Elephants Stir 47
Five	Elephants on the Rampage and Rebranding the Republicans 76
	Conclusion Elephants in the Forest 107
	About the Authors 121
	Citation Index 123

A Note to the Reader

Postmortems on the 2016 election will keep political analysts and scholars busy for years. And although I briefly discuss the 2016 Republican nominee Donald Trump, he is not the primary topic of this book. One of the questions that will be asked and answered many times, particularly on the Republican side is 'How did we get here?' How could a party ostensibly based in traditionally conservative ideals like limited government and free markets be made over as a populist nationalist movement based on a strong-man executive branch, protectionism and anti-immigration? This book attempts to layout the pathway that brought the American experiment to this juncture.

We the authors of this book are neither Republican nor Democrat, liberal nor conservative. We each adhere to aspects of both conservative and liberal "categories" of the political spectrum, and then some. So, we do not have a political agenda per se in writing this book. Both of us are committed to modern democratic republican forms of government. However, we both equally are committed to the idea that ancient democratic political thought and practices have something important to offer our own modern democratic republic here in the United States.

Our understanding that led to the messages that we present comes from knowledge of ancient democratic thought, especially from Aristotle, combined with our knowledge of modern republicanism and democratic theory, along with extensive studies and teaching of American politics, government, and culture. Our main message is simple and twofold: Firstly, every healthy political community needs an authentically conservative party or element, lively and vital, in order to secure the community's stability in the face of all other political parties that are movement oriented, using politics for political and social change. Americans usually associate such movement politics with progressivism and Progressives with "liberals" and the Democratic Party. Secondly, America's Republican Party as of now has lost any voice of authentic conservatives in America, being itself factionalized into what we call progressive conservatives, and then reactionaries, and extremists. The main or official voice that we hear from the GOP and the way the party presents itself are no longer authentically conservative. It is mostly progressive conservatism. Authentic conservatives have no real voice in America, no truly effective representation upon the political stage here. Thus, we no longer have the lively and vital conservative element required to ensure stability in the face of the progressive and reactionary movement politics on the right or the progressive movement politics of the left. Movement politics dominates our political landscape, domestically and in foreign policy.

Our first message, that every political community needs conservatives, comes largely from our understanding of Aristotle, along with a few other Ancients, and from modern analysts of these thinkers within a context of modern politics. Surprisingly, perhaps, we find ourselves more or less in harmony with what E. J. Dionne Jr. writes in *Our Divided Political Heart*: "every nation needs an intelligent and constructive form of conservatism . . . suspicious of innovation and therefore subject[s] all grand plans to merciless interrogation" for their effectiveness and for "unintended consequences." Reminiscent of Edmund Burke, Dionne reminds us that conservatives "respect old things and old habits." Acknowledging that it may not always be right to cling to these, nevertheless "our habits are the product of time, based on the slowly accumulated wisdom of our ancestors. That's why tradition should not be discarded lightly." Finally Dionne tells us that a third key value of conservatism to any nation is its "suspicion of human nature and a belief that people cannot be remolded like plastic. . . . Efforts to alter human nature, the conservative is right to insist, can risk descent into totalitarians catastrophe." We, in our own way, attempt here to amplify and explain Dionne's conclusion that "a society that fails to keep these conservative warnings in mind is likely to run into trouble."

We have written this book for every American citizen. We appeal here to your wisdom, rather than the so-called wisdom of the academic or scholar. We are practical average citizens engaged in the toils of daily life and all that goes with that. We ourselves are scholars in the sense that we are educated and experienced to be so. But we are not established in any one of the "ivory towers" of academia, but instead struggle for positions in our efforts to secure a living and hopes for permanency in our efforts as do many of you. One of us has worked as a professional journalist and in marketing after having worked at several of those jobs that one takes to work one's way through a university education. The other has taught at five universities in the United States and Canada over the past sixteen years, with a celebrated teaching career spanning twelve years at one of these universities here in the United States. This has been a second career, after a long stint as a truck mechanic, preceded by work as a car washer, gas jockey, busboy, and dishwasher, along with several intermittent "street jobs" along the way. We both have learned much from the school of hard knocks.

So, we share our thoughts and concerns with you, as two of you, writing these to you as best we can. We hope that you will consider well what we have to say. It is very important for us together to understand these things and to use that understanding as we listen to politicians and pundits so that we are not led astray by double talk, false speech, and the rest that resides within the political rhetoric to which we are subjected by those who wish to lead and govern us.

We speak here of the "ends of conservatism," not as the passing or demise of conservatism. Rather, the "ends of conservatism" are the purposes and meanings of conservative thought and action, their effects upon the political community. In *The Woven Figure*, George F. Will quotes American author John Dos Passos as having once wrote: "In the time of change and danger, when there is a quicksand of fear under ones's reasoning, a sense of continuity with generations before can stretch like a lifeline across the scary present." Wills tells us that "I do not know when Das Passos expressed that impeccably conservative sentiment, but it is certainly germane to the scary present." We do know that Wills published this in 1997. If times were scary then, they have only become scarier since, far scarier. Whatever the political leanings are of yourself and those around you, we all should respect and value authentic conservatism as a necessity in our own political arenas, local, state, and national. No matter how you may cast your vote at the ballot box, America needs a vital and lively authentic conservatism to thrive within our borders. And this authentic conservatism of which we speak needs an authentic voice, a true voice, in American politics.

Sara A. Jarman
Brent Gilchrist
July 2016

Introduction

Authentic Conservatism, Movement Conservatism and the Republican Party

Americans have always been a people set apart from the rest of the world. Our geographic location more or less guaranteed this, but the fact that we came into being as a people gathered around a compact set of ideas essentially ensured that we would remain a people apart. Other countries have nations—people born of the same soil, language, culture, and traditions. We have a republic—a *res publica* or one public person—united across different birthplaces, languages, cultures, and traditions by an idea of what it means to be American. *E pluribus unum*—out of many, one—has been a reality as well as an ideal throughout most of our history. Our "Ancient Founding" made this so, at least we are told that it was made for this possibility. But that thing that has become a nasty word—"politics"—is the thing that has kept it so. Politics has kept alive the continual struggle to become this one thing, this one realization of a singular idea that somehow seems more noble, more significant, and even more divine to many, than all of the previous struggles of human history put together. Our politics has made America great.

Politics is a human struggle to bring a single decision out of the clamor of many voices, to create out of the many demands and opinions surrounding any particular public concern a single and effective voice, in our case the voice of "we the people." This means, just as Aristotle said thousands of years ago, that politics is a good thing and not a "necessary evil" as many Americans more commonly believe today, many even thinking it is not so necessary and is just plainly evil.[1] In this book, we will explore this idea that politics is a good thing, even a necessary thing to human beings. Politics raises us above the animals with whom we share our existence upon the earth. This notion of the good of politics will emerge throughout the chapters of this book. Assuming for now, though, that this is the case—that we need politics and it is good—it must be that we need many voices to bring together these important human accomplishments that we call laws. Laws are the compromised and negotiated outcomes of the struggle for decisions by which we express our humanity. To struggle politically is to be human; Aristotle called us the "political animal." Of all the many voices and demands that we hear in American politics, those of the American conservative resound the existence of a peculiar yet massive group of citizens whose existence, like it or not, is absolutely necessary to the vitality of politics in our country and to the survival of the original idea of America as a people still set apart as a republic, one body politic, *res publica*.

Politics, in the common vernacular, often connotes a necessary evil that merely requires toleration; however, by its very nature, politics is a two-edged sword. Though often used to control and manipulate "the masses," the existence of politics is a necessary good as well, according to Hannah Arendt. She finds that "the answer to the question of the meaning of politics is so simple and conclusive that one might think that all the other answers are beside the point. The answer of politics is freedom." In both *The Human Condition* and *The Promise of Politics*, Arendt reminds her readers of a former understanding of the meaning of politics, while also attempting a revival of its principles. Although Arendt is skeptical of success for this political revival, considering the corruption that has consumed the political arena in modernity, she nonetheless aspires to reinvigorate modern politics with some original meaning and understanding. The realm of politics, she argues, originally provided for the highest form of human self-actualization,

Elephants on the Rampage

but has since been perverted by the merging of mankind's political and social lives. Private life and public life used to be practically distinct, one from another.[2] Household matters, enlarged and made public as social matters in modernity, were dealt with within the private life of the home. This is no longer true. Indeed, as Arendt notes, "in the modern world, the two realms indeed constantly flow into each other like waves in the never-resting stream of the life process itself. The disappearance of the gulf that the ancients had to cross daily to transcend the narrow realm of the household and 'rise' into the realm of politics is an essentially modern phenomena."[3] This entails the demise of the essence of politics, according to Arendt, a human tragedy scarcely noticed because of its gradual erosion over time.

Politics rises to the development of human virtues, talents, great deeds and speeches in which we "become" fully human beings above our private concerns, above society. We now have debased politics by consuming it with social matters, mistaking society for politics and overwhelming our public life with economics and other private matters of individual households collectivized into "public affairs."[4]

Arendt reminds us that for the Greeks "the household life spent in the privacy of 'one's own,' outside the world of the common is 'idiotic' by definition." Thus, our consuming the common or public life of politics with the collective lives of "one's own" as society has made our politics idiotic.[5] Household management, or economics, was something that could be mastered well enough to leave it behind to enter the political life of human beings by hiring managers to administer these private matters.[6] Administration of the household has now become collectively the administration of society, and with society overwhelming the political, we are now left with administration as the height of our public life. Politics has become administration. Our "politicians" are simply managers managing the economy and securing for us prosperity, including the comforts of staying alive better and longer.[7] We only have to consider how readily we determine good or successful presidencies with good economic times, for instance. All other modern politics bear this same character, more or less, at various levels of our "political" lives.

xv

Sara Jarman with Brent Gilchrist, Ph.D.

In the political realm, authentic conservatives are moderate people who by their very nature have a tendency to resist change. They are just made that way.[8] Here we first signal a difference between conservatives truly and those in name only, a distinction that separates Republicans into many categories with authentic conservatives being but one. Republicans now include among their ranks progressive conservatives. This group—like Lenin and Stalin along with all politicians who have "plans" or blueprints for change—have plans of reform and leaders who write books about themselves and their ideas. These ideas are always presented as "for the better," but history says something to the contrary each time those plans get implemented. Along with progressive conservatives, the Republican Party still contains a large group of reactionaries who would return America to 1776 overnight and thereby create a nightmare of a revolution now that's even worse than it was then. Most of us denote such Americans as "more conservative" even though they would change us to a far greater degree and much faster than any political group now existing, or ever previously existed, in our republic. Instead of being more conservative, these are radicals and revolutionaries. Hence, it is no wonder that they identify with the American Revolution and her "Patriots" and events such as the Boston Tea Party. These so-called conservatives are as radical and revolutionary on the right of the political world as are Communist revolutionaries on the left. Both groups would turn the world upside down without regard to costs and shocks to our political system.

Authentic conservatives fit somewhere in the middle of these extremes yet remain within the Republican Party. They appreciate what they have, where they have come from, and hope that where they are going will be much the same—a known world of predictability and outcomes whereby one can expect to reap what one has sown, for good or for ill.[9] Conservatives especially resist political change and big change at that. They would rather let alone those things that are accomplished by politics of grand designs and blueprints of hope. However, conservatives are not against change altogether. Of course they want to improve things where things may be improved. It is just that the known world is almost always better to them than the worlds that might emerge from unintended consequences that tag along like unseen parasites upon any great plans of political change, however well-intentioned those plans might be. No plan can account for the risks that might be borne within them. Conservatives are wary of these risks precisely because they cannot be known in advance. Therefore, they would rather try to improve the political world gradually through trial and error so that the costs of errors will not be so great and course corrections not so burdensome so as to be prevented altogether. The cure for any existing political ill should be known to not be worse than the disease. To act otherwise would plainly be quackery. Conservatives know that we have more than enough "politicians" standing at the crossroads selling "magic tonics" and "fixes everything" elixirs. They don't believe in such stuff and never have.[10]

This is not to say that conservatives fly by the seats of their pants—they do have plans. But these are moderate, unlike the grandiose visions of their ideological political opponents. Conservatives want to explore the political world with a certain humility and caution rather than go full steam ahead with a determination to stay a course come what may. The ship of state should move slowly, checking its course along the way and staying close to ports to repair and refit itself rather than setting off into the unknown upon the open sea of political troubles and turmoil that may end in celebrated success or in terrible tragedy. Conservatives naturally would rather avoid the risk of tragedy because the world they know is well enough that such risks seem unwarranted to them. We can improve ourselves more slowly, they argue, and move forward into the future carefully. In other words, conservatives would rather only tinker with government programs and policies than create grand new ones. They strive to preserve traditions and question or change them only with great hesitancy. They speak out against political movements regardless of the direction or purpose of those movements.[11]

For the aforementioned reasons, conservatives may appear to be obstinate at times when they stand against change in efforts to preserve the things they care about. This is especially true when proposed changes are big and quick. However, this obstinacy is a good of conservatism, one of its ends—the goals and purposes of authentic conservatism that we will explore in what follows. Some of the hallmarks of conservatism include its willingness to listen to proposals and negotiate careful and thoughtful change that keeps us connected to our past even as we venture into the future. In other words, the limits and possibilities of the ends of conservatism are political. Conservatism involves certain attitudes and approaches of engaging the political world and its demands so that we have one voice to represent the many as we struggle toward good policies and practices together as a people. Conservatives are not merely one small or even equal voice among the many in America; however, "a large majority of Americans are conservatives" of the authentic type that we are describing with an attachment to existing society that stands up for its legitimacy against those who would change things dramatically.[12] Thus, we have a critical mass for stability in the political world that allows us to entertain change without giving ourselves wholly over to it wantonly.

In this book, we strive to clarify that the political ends of authentic American conservatism may keep our politics lively and changeable upon a foundation of the past. Thus, conservatives provide an important vitality that distinguishes them from their cousins of close resemblance within the Republican Party, those elephants on the rampage to the left and to the right of them who keep conservatives "stuck in the middle" of the Grand Old Party that is increasingly open to change while becoming more dogmatic. Republicans are becoming less a political party than a loose assemblage of peoples on the right of the political spectrum in America that are barely held together by the fact that they all call themselves conservative, but nearly driven apart by those on the move either progressively or radically as reactionaries. Conservatives in name only, these are the party's elephants on the rampage, trampling the past and the present into rubble that becomes awkward, inconvenient truths on their blazing trails of change.

In the modern age, all voices for political change, other than those of authentic conservatives, originate out of mass movements with plans for rapid departures from the past and even from the status quo. Modern conservatism was born as a response to such political movements.[13] Originally, its response was just to keep things as they were. This was unacceptable to all other plans for political change, or "ideologies," as they have come to be called. One by one, these ideologies gained enough followers and popularity to turn their political beliefs and plans into political power with enough momentum to overcome conservative resistance, sometimes in long drawn out processes and at other times in revolutions of great and rapid change.

Since the basis of political power for these ideologies is popular appeal, and since this popular appeal is based upon promises to the people of change and hope, each of these ideologies persists in creating plans for the future betterment of the people. An ideological movement cannot simply overthrow old governments, gain power, and then come to rest. It must continue to move, to promise progress and change for the good in order to keep the support of their followers lively and active. All ideologies continue to be movement oriented, always directing their citizens towards a better tomorrow.[14]

In America, our liberal democracy was on the move throughout the Nineteenth Century, settling the West by building railroads and industry and the cities that go along with them. The American Dream seemed to be appearing before our eyes, self-evident in its possibilities and accomplishments. It was as if everyone could be on the move whether geographically, economically, or morally. We had the stuff of our own improvement in our independence both individually and as a people. Individualism became rugged in these years of struggling on the frontier.[15] When our Declaration of Independence was subliminally written into the Constitution with the blood of the Civil War, the words of Lincoln's Gettysburg Address, and the ink of the Civil War Amendments, freedom and equality became great partners in the American project. Both ideals struggle for supremacy in the hearts and minds of our people at times; nevertheless, both reside in America's soul perpetually. The rugged individualism of our practical experience gained political significance as citizenship came to mean something to every American and equality became a watchword with new meaning in a country that no longer held slaves in bondage.[16]

But words and dreams are always grander than the realities that they try to describe. By the end of the Nineteenth Century and moving into the Twentieth Century, big business and industry had made things tough on urban workers who had nowhere else to go in the new America. Their ability to strike out on their own was hampered by the already accomplished settling of the frontier. No longer could one say, as did Horace Greely, "Go West, young man!"[17] Additionally, trusts and monopolies had done their work to ensure the hardest years of Industrial Capitalism were not so hard for the few but very difficult indeed for the many. Unable to move outward geographically or upward economically any longer, the Great Unwashed in America began to move on their own both socially and politically. Populist movements arose in rural areas as farmers struggled to better their lot through political organization and movement.[18] Progressives emerged out of moderate elements, in both the Republican and Democratic parties, as a political movement in urban areas on behalf of industrial workers everywhere. Republican participation with progressivism was short-lived, however, with Theodore Roosevelt's presidency signaling its high water mark within the GOP. Being absorbed by the Democrats instead, progressivism began to dominate American politics with continual demands and movements for progress. We have remained on the move to this day with progressive politics as a permanent feature of America's political landscape.[19]

Early twentieth-century reforms seemed to promise enough progress for mainstream Americans; the lot of everyone was improved, at least in theory. President Woodrow Wilson was a political scientist, after all. He came up with plans and set them in place for America's continuing progress according to scientific knowledge and blueprints of political architecture. The Republic would be reformed by progressive politics, which is to say by modern scientific and rational planning of overhauling the institutions of government and even the meaning of the Constitution of the country itself.[20]

It is this prolonged persistence of twentieth-century progressive politics that gave birth to American conservatism as we know it today. With politics existing as the struggle between alternate voices, the first and most obvious political voice to emerge against our prolonged progressivism was the conservative cry to stop all this political movement, all this change. President Herbert Hoover represents the old conservatives who tried to stand against the onslaught of political change that was to come eventually with Franklin Roosevelt's New Deal. Hoover insisted, along with other conservatives of the "old school," that things were just not that bad, and that dramatic change was unnecessary and dangerous.[21] This was a stereotype of an antiquated American conservatism that first responded to modern progressivism, a conservatism of nay-saying and standing still. But things got worse and change was inevitable.

The crises of the 1930s and 1940s—the Great Depression and World War II—kept demands upon government to act and to act aggressively. The economy and national security became the focus of these demands and of government activity in these decades and on into the Cold War and the 1950s. This concentration of government action upon basic social interests of economics and security, both initially and upon other social issues altogether, will be of concern to us throughout this book as well. We will wonder with you if this is politics at all or some other form of power and authority to which we have become increasingly subject.

After decades of progressive politics and government by Democratic Presidents, Republican Dwight "Ike" Eisenhower presided over the 1950s with a grandfatherly aura that now seems to us as though it exuded American conservatism in government and public life. The Republican Party seemed to represent mainstream Americans with its conservative agenda of preserving a "way of life" for all Americans.[22] This was all that was needed to keep the Party and its members close to the hearts of average Americans—these dreamers of the American Dream, whoever they might be. Even after the Democrats had been the ones to apparently pull us out of the Great Depression and the Second World War, Ike and the Republicans gave us America's glory days of middle class suburbs, indoor plumbing, and modern appliances for all. Televisions began to glow from every home instead of the primitive embers of fireplaces that marked a time long gone. Everything was becoming modern, secured by the Republican Party that conserved the liberty of the American Constitution upon which all things good were predicated. Its separation of powers were the "Mainspring of Human Progress," according to a top executive of General Motors in his book published under that title. And that mainspring seemed to be guarded vigilantly by Republican politicians guaranteeing our "way of life" long into the future.[23]

Americans, at least good Americans, had a "way of life" whereas others had ideologies and political programs for change and supposed progress. Other modern societies had ideologies, but not Americans.[24] That's why politics and progress made by others looked entirely different to us than the America we had come to know and love. With equality for all and liberty for only a few, ideologies were foreign to Americans. Instead, we had what we thought was the science of modern progressivism and its reforms. What began as piecemeal programs became increasingly organized programs under the rational planning of the New Deal and later within the rising military-industrial complex and its burgeoning bureaucracy. We were working out the kinks of rational planning and preparing ourselves for a new America even under the Eisenhower administration.[25] "Renegade" conservatives, even some working within the administration, labeled Ike's politics as "progressive conservatism" because his administration continued the growth of government that came before it and followed its rational blueprinting of change and progress more or less continuously.[26] Disgruntled conservatives in the administration and the party spoke out against Ike, publishing books about true conservatism and some going so far as to call Ike a communist for some of the progressive policies emerging under his administration.[27] Government was growing, and with it American power was being centralized into the hands of fewer and fewer people who had narrow interests of their own to pursue and protect rather than the national interest. President Eisenhower warned the country about this in his Farewell Address and called us to vigilance against falling prey to the very machinery of government and the "military industrial complex" that he had helped to create.[28]

Elephants on the Rampage

It is this era and its politics that gave birth finally to modern conservatives and to the supposed conservative movement that we think we know today. Authentic conservatives emerged as Republicans complaining in response to their own party's movement politics and to their progressive conservatism as a mirror of the Democratic politics they opposed. These authentic American conservatives opposed movement politics by Democrats and Republicans alike. But with everyone else on the move to a better future, with all politics surrounding them being progressive in one form or another, it was as though these conservatives were alone crying in the wilderness.

Out of these politics, a so-called "conservative movement" emerged through the late 1950s and into the 1960s, eventually spitting up Barry Goldwater as a candidate for the presidency in 1964. Goldwater was very close to being an authentic conservative but not quite. His participation in a movement and his acceptance (or rather tolerance for lack of a better candidate) by the Republican Party as their candidate disqualify him as authentically conservative. This did, however present America with an apparent alternative to progressive politics, or movements of the left, with a new movement on the right. It was something different from the progressive conservatism of the mainstream Republican moderates who had been competing with the Democrats on their own ground.[29]

Not only did Goldwater's apparently conservative movement seem to give a new voice and hope to truly conservative Americans by finally putting conservatives on this competitive political ground too, but it also gave political birth to Ronald Reagan and his future conservative movement. This finally would bear fruit to the long stifled voices of the Republican center, the heart and soul of the party and the apparent heart and soul of America under Reagan's presidency too. It was as if the Republican Party was midwife to Goldwater as he gave life to the son of America (Reagan) who would rise to the apogee of American "conservatism" out of the pains and political death of Goldwater's labors. Of all of Barry Goldwater's accomplishments, the one that stands most important in memory of the movement, was Ronald Reagan's rise to the presidency.

Sara Jarman with Brent Gilchrist, Ph.D.

Of course, this did not happen overnight, nor simply from the conservative movement of the 1960s. Reagan had to make the movement his own with some political and cultural help. The turmoil and politics of the 1960s and the disaster that was the Vietnam War might have been enough for Americans to look for a president who could lift their spirits once more. However, with Watergate and Nixon's resignation a Republican president who was far from conservative and therefore far from acceptable, was followed by the responding Democratic President Jimmy Carter. Americans wanted to feel good about themselves once more.[30]

With perfect timing, the 1973 movie "American Graffiti" became a big hit then the spin-off television show "Happy Days" lit up every home in America weekly. Both of these pop culture phenomena created a growing nostalgia for the 1950s and those "good old days" with grandfather President Ike. Music, clothing styles, haircuts and makeup all emulated those happy days of our imaginations, although updated with a certain flare of knowing or cynical nostalgia. Only an actor like Reagan could bring this nostalgia to life politically and into the White House, and this could happen only on the back of Goldwater and his earlier work to set up this supposedly conservative movement. Conservatives now have a nostalgia for the Reagan era as the Golden Age of American politics, emulating the nostalgia that brought Reagan into the White House in the first place. But Reagan was no conservative. During his tenure he grew big government, added huge deficits to the national debt, made radical Executive actions against our own in labor disputes and in foreign affairs such as the Iran-Contra scandal, and signaled an unbelievable faith in science and rational planning on a global scale with his Star Wars defense plans. He pursued a very progressive conservatism that was made palpable by the actual investments in utopian planning. Reagan spoke like a conservative but governed like a progressive conservative of the mainstream Republican Party. It is no wonder he was so popular and is remembered with such reverence by conservatives of every stripe. Reagan played the role of a multifaceted character of broad appeal and played the part well—it was the best role of his career.

Elephants on the Rampage

Since Reagan, we have had a comedy of errors amongst those claiming to be conservative. Newt Gingrich's "Contract with America" is precisely the sort of ideological tract and planning that one would expect from the early Soviets and their ideological salesmanship of themselves as leaders of progress and rational planning. His book is only surpassed by his later claims during presidential debates as he vied to become the contender against President Obama. While Gingrich claimed to be the only conservative on a stage of six or seven Republican candidates for the presidential nomination, he also spoke of plans to colonize the moon. If any other candidate had announced such plans, we would have laughed him off, but Gingrich asserted his seriousness and rebuked doubters. Clearly, Newt Gingrich has progressive planning in his DNA and is anything but conservative.[31] George W. Bush's presidency can be seen as progressive conservatism as well with "no child left behind." It was a blueprint for education in America and an intervention into state and local education that exemplifies rational planning imposed upon people like a road map that doesn't fit the diverse topography across the nation. And in the end, "no child left behind" became a thorn in the side of educators everywhere. Clearly, we have seen nothing but progressive conservatism coming from the Republicans, so much so that authentic conservatives have been lured by the siren's song of the Tea Party that has emerged on their right.[32]

The Tea Party is not a conservative movement, nor a progressive conservative movement, but is a reactionary response to their own Republican Party having been bogged down in its own progressive conservatism pursued in tandem with the Democrats. Tea Partiers want change and want out of the politics of the status quo. However, they are involved in movement politics enough to disqualify them as authentically conservative. The difference is that their movement is backwards with an eye on a "Golden Age" of America's Founding. This, we will show, is reactionary and utopian rather than conservative. Any such movement is as radical on the right as would be a socialist or communist revolutionary movement on the left. The radical revolutionary upheaval of the country at hand, whether on the left or on the right, can in no way be considered conservative because both call for rapidly change institutions and practices to adhere to an ideal. However, Tea Partiers catch the attention of authentic conservatives both because the party speaks a language of values that resonates with conservatives and because these same conservatives are disillusioned with the progressive conservatism to the left of their party. The progressive conservatism dominates the Republicans as they try to appeal to voters and compete with Democrats again on the Democrats' ground instead of upon conservative principles and policies.[33]

Conservative Americans are now having an increasingly difficult time defining what their ideology means. The Republican Party seems at odds with itself and in an inner struggle to understand itself then somehow communicate this to the American electorate. Republicans now ask themselves questions about how to get elected and what policies and programs to adopt to appeal to those segments of the population that are lost to them. However, it is clear that they seem willing to advocate any movement or plans that might bolster their chances for winning elections. They have now gone so far as to create questionnaires designed for the public to tell them what the Republican Party should stand for, even targeting particular segments of the population exclusively to gain appeal for them in upcoming elections. The progressive conservatives who now dominate the right are trying to keep up with the Democrats and compete with them ideologically for the same voters. These Republicans struggle to develop the plans and prescriptions of a sustainable ideology for the immediate future and its upcoming elections. Their plans, movement and policies of change toward a better future for "all Americans" rather than their principles will be the ground upon which they stand to call for voters to rally to their cause

Authentic conservatism is not an ideology. In fact, authentic conservatives reject the legitimacy of all ideologies entirely. Currently, Republicans that claim conservatism typically embrace plans for change that are progressive. They prescribe movement politics that are characteristic of ideological change, which elicits greater change at faster rates than typical of traditional political evolution. Ideologies—or blueprints for change—enable speedy and radical overhauls of politics and government according to prescribed patterns of mass appeal. They tend toward movements, and all ideological movements tend toward destabilizing societies and politics with change that is foreign to their traditions and constitutions. Conservative change is gradual and evolutionary, which is more authentically representative of the people themselves.[34]

Ideological politics and progressive methods of government are supposed to be foreign to conservatives. Thus, American conservatives are engaged in a psychological as well as a practical identity crisis leaving the Democrats only dealing with pragmatic problems typical of them. In response to its own crises, "conservatism" has increasingly become more progressive in attempts to redefine itself as a political ideology to maintain relevancy and legitimacy amongst the general public. When both parties use progressive tactics to accomplish their ends, which for both are now merely winning elections, we can only expect gridlock as both sides are entrenched in mirror images of each other. Or we will see instability emerge as breakout parties, like the Tea Party could become, that may arise in response to the gridlock and express the frustration of American citizens with the status quo. More recently, the emergence and success of a non-traditional presidential candidate like Donald Trump has occurred because of a fractured Republican Party's failure to be true to its inherent conservative identity. Americans are used to political movements and expect change and progress now, and authentic conservatism has become nearly invisible on our political landscape.

We argue that conservatism is necessary within modern society, especially within American society because its founding was at least partially rooted in the classical past, and classical societies believed strongly in maintaining an active political community. Ours is a conservative appeal to the past for the sake of conservatism in the present. Ultimately, our appeal for conservatism is intended to serve the end of political balance. We advocate the necessity of true conservatism within a polity, not because we hold conservative tenets to be true, or because we are conservative, but because we maintain that a sufficient element of society must be truly conservative for balance to be maintained, both for political stability and the health of the polity. Ultimately, it is balance or moderation that is our cause.

One

Conservatism as an Ideology

In America, usually to say "Republican" is to think "conservative," and to say "conservative" is to think "Republican." It was not always this way. The Republican Party originally emerged before the Civil War out of a coalition of businessmen, reformers, and radicals looking for a tradition to make them and some of their radical politics seem legitimate to fellow Americans at that time. Some of their politics included such extreme policies as freeing slaves and even living side by-side with them as citizens afterwards. Moderate Republicans—businessman, bankers, and lawyers—combined forces with the radicals to emerge as a national force to challenge America's prevailing status quo, which was defended by the Democrats.[35] So by default, the Democrats were the conservative party of the day. Eventually, the Republicans would become known throughout American history as the party of Lincoln, which meant the party of freedom to many Americans. Lincoln was the man who could bring movement and change to a country in gridlock between two great sections. Even if it was to come through civil war rather than democratic politics, Lincoln would still be able to bless us with a legitimate new tradition, or a "new birth of freedom," through his renewed emphasis upon the values of the Declaration of Independence. These became our values too. The Declaration would become equal with the Constitution as a founding document for most Americans.[36] So it is that in the early days of Republican politics, the main business elements of the party and their supporters simply tried to use the reformers and radicals so their party could to gain power and forge this new tradition. Only later would they then be tasked to conserve this tradition for us, and the Republicans eventually became associated with conservatism and known typically as the conservative party.

The American Dream was given new meaning as equality of opportunity came to the new frontier when the West was opened for settlement after the war. For average Americans, as well as for the sorts of men who are always on the move, the West presented a stage upon which the American Dream could be played out as both image and reality in a land where one could "get rich quick." These images and the "American Way of Life" they represented became the background for the Republican Party, which settled into the Twentieth Century as the conservative party designated to protect what had now become "traditional" America.

After World War II, America's own original, Russell Kirk, tried to help shape our understanding of American conservatism as an idea. He wrote that conservatism didn't really exist until England's Edmund Burke wrote his *Reflections on the Revolution in France*. Burke used his commentary on the French Revolution to create a political theory of modern conservatism.[37] He didn't just argue against the excesses of the French Revolution and the reign of terror that included all those heads lopped off into baskets in front of cheering crowds. He argued that conservatism would be necessary in any political society in order to resist such chaos and instability. Conservatism came into being as essentially anti-ideology, applicable in opposition to any ideology in any historical or political circumstance in which ideology is working toward social and political change. In cases wherein all other voices are calling for change, conservatism becomes the only alternative voice against these movement politics, the only hold upon the grounds of stability and, the only real choice against movement, the very element that keeps politics alive. Herein we see conservatism not as mere prejudice favoring tradition, but as reflection defending our inherited condition against pressures from and for political movement of all directions, speed, and type. By its nature, conservatism sets off warning bells to alert us to what we have to lose with various changes being proposed or forced upon us. Its political task is to help us remember and to weigh and measure the value of our circumstance before we abandon it to promises of goods that dwell in the unknown.[38] In our current circumstances, we should remember that America's modern conservatism just might have a role to play in connection with the prolonged progressivism that we have experienced. Perhaps conservative reflection can renew questions about these changes, and by the very asking of such questions, revive politics in America. Authentic conservative reflection may arouse us from our rest upon the technical administration of progress by governments that are always on the move, or trying to be on the move.

Burke emphasized the good of conservatism by contrasting it with the fatal consequences of excessive liberalism in the French Revolution. Implicit in his argument is a denunciation of all movement politics and of modern ideologies that drive these movements. He argued that in the heat of ideological passion, people are liable to support policies they otherwise would not entertain let alone act upon. Filled with hope and belief, they help shape movements of rapid political change. To balance out ideological passion, Burke theorized conservatives would build and rebuild governments and political institutions patiently and with proper reason moderated by the practices and our traditions that history has given to us. Burke saw that the French Revolutionaries chased after liberty according to ideological plans of movement politics. Instead, they actually found their own despotic reign. He realized that in order for liberty to truly take root within society it could not come from ideological revolutions and political movements unleashed from any opposition. Instead, liberty could only really come to us through gradually evolving social norms and institutions.[39] Such caution and wisdom characterize conservatism as a response to these modern politics of foundation shaking movements. So began modern American conservatism in the middle of the Twentieth Century as a voice of constancy ready to resist progressivism and its scientific planning for a better society.

Ideology had always been a bad word in America. Soviets, communists, socialists, and fascists had ideologies. We had an American way of life, and with it an American way of thinking. When prominent academics wrote about Soviet and American politics, they consistently called Soviet thinking ideology but never used this word for American "thought."[40] We spoke of ideology, especially communist ideology, as a "secular religion." This is an oxymoron because if it's a religion, it's not secular, and if secular then it's not religion. But, the effect of words and phrases matters more in American politics than precise meanings and logical consistency. Political rhetoric moves the hearts and minds of the people with talk that they understand and already believe implicitly. Additionally, they can be persuaded to believe they already know the things that politicians tell them, that they already have a deep conviction of the things that they hear. We are attached to our principles as truths, which is self-evident from our beginnings.

As academics are prone to do, however, they make things more complicated for the rest of us. They started to clean up ideology as a concept, as sets of ideas that all of us could have and use, even conservatives. In 1957, Samuel Huntington—prominent American political scientist and one time President of the American Political Science Association—wrote an article called "Conservatism as an Ideology" about how conservatives too could have an ideology. With this, Huntington assigned to conservatives the thing which they always had been defined against. Now conservatism could be a movement too. Now they could have plans, make policy blueprints for progress, and speak of their conservative ideology alongside liberals and socialists and all those supposed relevant politicians and ideas and movements. Now conservatives could move out of the shadows of liberal democrats and all their progressive accomplishments of the first half of the Twentieth Century. Conservatives could become relevant once more, maybe even attractive, to American voters and their increasingly modern sensibilities. We all want progress, after all. Even American conservatives want some sort of change, improvement, and accomplishment of the

Elephants on the Rampage

American Dream. Now, conservatives could have plans, present programs of action, and appeal to American voters that their course into the future was the right one.[41] At about the same time in the mid-1950s, Russell Kirk was writing against ideology as political fanaticism. Kirk held that deep convictions cannot easily be put into words, but these "principles as rules of life and politics" in America are lived daily. We do not need ideology, he argues, to narrow these into small and specific words of manipulation and degradation of human grandeur of the heart and mind.[42] Nevertheless, Huntington said that conservatism could be rational enough to fit itself into the organized thinking of competing ideologies so that conservatives could keep up with the changing times. It seemed that the "American Way of Life" was giving way to the rational planning that characterized foreign ideologies and also characterized our own governments at home. We now needed ways to think about and plan for changes and the administration of our own politics and governments. It no longer sufficed to merely describe politics; we now had to plan and arrange the political world around us, gifted as we think we are with modern science as truth.[43]

The same rational planning that was going into government programs and advances in science and technology gave rise to a new heyday in the dominance of American Political Science. Rather than giving increasingly complex and accurate descriptions of the political world, as they had been doing in really big books, political scientists began to work more and more toward perfecting their scientific and mathematical abilities to describe with minute accuracy our political activity. They have done this so that they could bring their social science into the modern age alongside other "hard" sciences, like physics and mathematics, in order to gain equal respect as tellers of truth. It should be noted here that this struggle and ambition continues.[44] In 2013, Senator Tom Coburn of Oklahoma tried to have National Science Foundation funding removed from political science in universities throughout the United States because he believes that it is not truly scientific.[45] Political scientists work away at trying to become more and more scientific as if modern technical science is the way to find and judge all truth. But this new scientism cannot tell us that the U.S.

Constitution is divine, inspired, or even wise. Science has not determined when human life begins in the womb or what our duties are to one another as human beings or as fellow citizens. So modern American conservatism has become another voice for change according to its versions of scientific truths; it's yet another ideology to be opposed by authentic conservatives, even when dwelling within the same political party. Authentic conservatives strive to be heard and have effect within the Republican Party of progressive conservatives, reactionary libertarians, and radical Tea Partiers as if all are equally "conservative." They are not.

Such matters immediately above are subject to debate because they cannot be resolved by any truths delivered by modern scientism. As political issues, we must begin our examination of each of these issues from where we are and from the ground upon which our present understanding rests. As different groups desire things to be different, political movement emerges to shift this ground from underneath our feet. Sometimes we can, in fact, change to an improved position, but sometimes we may create more problems than we fix with, when we change rapidly and dramatically. Obviously, we can see a role for conservatism here to question the questioners of our inheritance, to ask movements toward the good to move slowly and thoughtfully, and to give to us a proper accounting of our accomplishments.

In fact, liberals in America's Democratic Party had been resisting conservatism consistently and successfully maintaining their movement politics since the Progressive movement and its earliest Republican teachers of our twentieth-century reforms. While the Republican Party stutter-stepped its way into the Twentieth Century with unorganized and relatively ad hoc progressive reforms for a time, the Democratic Progressives and New Dealers had learned to move beyond stutter steps and into advanced rational planning. This turned American liberalism into a progressive ideology that is every bit as lucid and prescriptive as any foreign ideology.[46] However, liberal progressivism was homespun and shaped and proven by our own experience. As we pushed toward the 1960s, American conservatism already began to look backward and old-fashioned. We needed plans and avenues to the future as we approached the conquest of new frontiers, not conservation of old ways and habits. Progress was the name of the day once more. Republicans knew this every bit as much as did the Democrats, and they had been working at it the same way as their opponents were.[47]

Originally, the mainstream of the Republican Party used the movement-oriented reformers and radicals to join them in electing the longshot candidate Abraham Lincoln to the presidency, but by the middle of the Twentieth Century, the modern rationalists and reformers had turned the tables and began to dominate the party and use its mainstream. Now it was the progressives' turn to use the conservatives in the party for legitimacy and electoral support as they appealed to Republican voters for elections while implementing their own new version of "progressive conservatism" for policy and governance. "Modern Republicanism" now dominated the party with its "moderate conservatism." It resembled the Democrats' progressivism too much for the likes of Barry Goldwater and Phyllis Schlafly who became famous as mainstays of Republican conservatism.[48] Now these conservatives were surrounded by Republicans on their left who embraced big government and blueprints for reform (anathema to authentic conservatives) and on their right by radical reactionaries who would soon sound the alarm for a return to 1776. The movement would grow with ebbs and tides over the next fifty years, culminating in the recent Tea Party movement and eventually—Donald Trump. Being farther on the right, these reactionaries are typically called more conservative when in fact they are radical revolutionaries who would throw government and society into unbelievable upheaval should they ever have their way. These and other far-right, movement-oriented radicals are merely necessary evils to the progressive conservatives on the left who have lately dominated the Republican Party. If elections didn't matter then these louder voices on the farther fringes could be ignored more openly than only being ignored quietly by those who matter in the Party.[49]

With both political parties in America organized as political movements—appealing to the same populace for election and increasingly focusing upon an undecided middle with promises of progressive liberalism or progressive conservatism—there came to be little difference between the two over time. Even when there were important matters of difference, voters were still faced with only a choice between different movements from movement politics. When movement politics is the only active polity in the country, there are clear signals that Americans are losing an authentic conservatism voice and connections to their political roots. "If a people forget their principles," Kirk says, "they relapse into barbarism and savagery. If a people reject sound principles for false principles, they become a nation of fanatics."[50]

The current fanaticism is all about movement. Promises of a brighter future or a better tomorrow signaled the narrow differences of real policies, the lack of real choice, and the appeal to Americans of novelty, of being on the move, of feeling as if we were still going somewhere into a new horizon. New frontiers were dished up for us to conquer as a country on the move both in reality and in virtual reality. Space was never the "final frontier" that we thought it was if American entrepreneurs could still attack the "Velcro frontier" or soccer moms could drive their kids around in Ford Frontiers.[51] This civilized isolation is a barbarism and frontierism of a second sort. It's not beastly struggles of life and death, but it's a loneliness and selfishness of civilized fragmentation one from another in a sort of sad resignation. The savagery to which Russell Kirk refers in this context is of a softer sort too, akin to the soft despotism that Tocqueville predicted for Americans long ago.[52]

Without diverse voices clamoring for that singular compromise from among the many and differing demands upon government, the lack of real choice meant the approach of the death of politics in America. Conservatives saw this problem emerging as early as the Eisenhower administration,[53] but even Aristotle had warned about it thousands of years ago. He taught that stable states required a diversity of interests and approaches to their political demands. James Madison built upon this idea in America when he argued that we could have a large republic. Since republics are a one-body politic, it was thought by many in America that we could not have a large republic, that we could not become one out of many.

Elephants on the Rampage

But Madison argued that the many would guarantee stability here by not allowing any one large faction to gain control of government power under our Constitution. Freedom, the real American value, would be guaranteed by the stability created with competing interests; in other words, a stability created by American politics.[54]

Conservatives in the Republican Party and within Eisenhower's own administration began to complain that the two parties, Democrats and Republicans, were resembling one another more and more all the time. They feared the lack of real choice in America and, therefore, the death of politics. Complaints were lodged against Eisenhower himself, saying that he was not conservative. Critics even went so far as to accuse him of being a communist in those days of wild accusations and name-calling that really could hurt you more than sticks and stones.[55] In reality, Ike was guided by a personal political philosophy of moderate conservatism blended with touches of liberalism. He had supported most of the New Deal measures, even later campaigning against the son of President Taft, Senator Robert A. Taft, who was the contemporary leader of conservative opposition to the New Deal. Senator Taft pledged to roll back the entire New Deal while President Eisenhower's administration went on to dismantle none of the social programs created by Roosevelt and Truman. It would have been revolutionary havoc to undo the New Deal. Eisenhower knew this and acted accordingly. Nevertheless, a Taft delegate predicted that Ike's election meant "eight more years of socialism."[56]

Ike's lack of commitment to the newly emerging conservative ideology meant that he was open-minded enough to take political advice from liberals. With this liberal influence, Eisenhower appointed Earl Warren Chief Justice of the Supreme Court and embraced Secretary Oveta Culp Hobby's policy of distributing the new polio vaccine universally throughout America at no cost to the people. This vaccine policy invited enough attacks against Hobby for advocating "socialized medicine" that she ultimately lost her job.[57] Eisenhower had his own grand plans that marked him as less than conservative as well. His ATOMS FOR PEACE plans were as half-baked as were his distant heirs' plans for "Star Wars," but they were frightening for their immediate reality of using nuclear weapons to create new harbors in Alaska or release trapped oil deposits, for instance.[58]

Eisenhower's Undersecretary of Labor from 1954 to 1956 and top speech writer from 1957 to 1958, Arthur Larson, was the Republican Party's best-spokesperson during the Eisenhower years. His book, *A Republican Looks at His Party*, a knock-off of Dean Acheson's *A Democrat Looks at His Party*, portrayed Ike's views of government and its relationship to the people as being much the same as the Democrats' views: government was the sum total of the people doing for the people what had to be done through the proper organization and assertion of power through the federal government whenever necessary.[59] Larson's book reminded Americans that they were born in revolt against traditional European conservatism and were now conserving principles born in that Revolution, beginning with the motto that "all men are created equal" and going on to conserve equality, anti-big government sentiments, states' rights, the peoples' rights, opposition to any concentration of power, and being against the existence of classes and class conflict.[60] Barry Goldwater would later say that this book was "an elaborate rationalization of 'Modern Republicanism'" or progressive conservatism.[61]

These new conservatives emerged precisely to address this need for a language of politics and change that could be used to appeal to American voters with a perspective on the right. This would thereby break the monopoly on such language and movement politics that had been held by the American left for so long. There is a paradox here that involves taking on non-conservative or even anti-conservative means to win elections and political power for the sake of empowering conservative values of an apparently sacred tradition. These sorts of mental and moral gymnastics are the province of the young, for the most part, so we saw a 25-year-old William Buckley Jr. emerging as a key leader amongst the new right.[62] Rather than seeking political power, however, Buckley pursued what might be seen as a moral high ground upon which he could acquire a different sort of power and influence. Buckley sought different outcomes than those he might have pursued as a politician. As an author of books and publisher of a major new conservative magazine, Buckley's influence was far broader and much more permanent than any series of votes on policies and legislation in which a politician might participate throughout an entire political career.[63]

Buckley became part of a new conservatism that focused largely upon economic issues that emerged out of the New Deal, including complaints about extensions of power by the federal government and the overreaching of its roles and responsibilities. This new conservatism touched upon morality only tangentially for the most part. Buckley remained an exception to this trend as an astute observer of American politics and of moral questions from the beginning, having first published his book *God and Man at Yale* as a young graduate, which denounced the atheism and socialism that he saw pervading the teaching at his alma mater.[64] In the *National Review*, his new influential magazine, we witness Buckley's fine political sensibilities as he complains that lacking truly distinct choices amongst America's movement politics is a blow to American freedom. Party members with different ideas are kicked out of the Republican Party, so Buckley complains of a party that has lost its identity, imagination, and creativity. Buckley sees in the Democrats and Republicans two parties that are so closely similar that competition between them is absent and identification by citizens with one or the other of them is impossible without any competitive sensibility. The essence of our party system is lost and with it the essence of politics in America. Buckley's is an early announcement of the death of politics in America, but it's also a call to its resurrection. Buckley sees that resurrection from America's decline from "strength, determination, and righteousness" to "wallowing in self-indulgence, decadence, and denial" can only come through politics.[65]

The seeking of a new conservatism to counter socialist and progressive ideologies on the left and extremist "conservative" philosophies on the right was sought by many as the salvation of Western civilization itself. This tended to place new conservatives of the business class and its rationalistic decision making processes at odds with traditional conservative interests in America. Big business also tended to be friendly with big government, another contrariness to be contained by 'conservatives' now of different stripes within the Republican Party. While some would answer this problem with a pragmatic sacrifice of ideological purity, giving up some non-essential conservative values for the sake of gaining political relevance, Buckley's magazine would publish moderate and realistic accounts of conservative life that stressed "small-town life, the simple virtues, hostility to the unions, to the intellectuals, to big government, and so on." Buckley worked to fill a void, the lack of any conservative voice against the liberal ideology of progressivism that had become intellectual and cultural dogma by the early 1960s. His *National Review* became that voice, the voice of a deliberately rootless kind of conservatism connected instead to liberalism as its enemy. The practical art of politics with its flexibility and yet conservative stability would seek the common good of a truly vibrant life of community, changing from authentic conservatives of the past without abandoning its basic principles.[66] All this was seen as futile because conservatives had no program, no ideological coherence and continuity, and no blueprint to guide policy and political action.

Thus it was that at the Republican Convention of 1964 the majority of delegates wanted some new kind of conservative. Although taking the nomination practically by default, Goldwater's acceptance speech announced that his candidacy would offer "a choice not an echo," which was a nod of disdain toward the Republicans' progressive conservatives who so closely shadowed their Democratic counterparts.[67], However, with Goldwater being a reluctant and entirely non-ideological candidate for the Party, Goldwater distanced himself from Buckley and the *National Review*. He ridiculed Eisenhower's domestic policies as a "dime store New Deal" while claiming to have gained his own conservatism not "through reading but rather through his experience as a small-town Western businessman and as a patriot in World War II."[68] Goldwater's was a "pragmatic" and not an "ideological" conservatism. Despite his differences with Eisenhower, Goldwater had been a loyal Republican, had "criticized New York Conservatives for setting up a Conservative Party" in 1962, and had kept his distance from Buckley's group because he resented the pressure placed upon him for the candidacy before he felt he was ready.[69] Showing his moderate nature, Goldwater tried to move the campaign to the center and kept the *National Review* out of the campaign since Buckley saw Goldwater as representing the "far mad right." Goldwater would not appear with Buckley at any time throughout the campaign.[70] Ronald Reagan, the ultimate winner in 1980 of Goldwater's 1964 campaign and these early conservative movements for power, was also distanced from Goldwater during the campaign. In fact, Goldwater and Regan were to make a promotional film together for national television, but it was called off because of Reagan's stance against social security and the damage that might do to the campaign, which was another signal of the moderate placement of himself that was sought after by Goldwater.[71]

Some Republican leaders had labeled themselves "progressive conservatives."[72] These Goldwater renounced outright as well as Larson's book reflecting upon the Party from the inside, which Goldwater denounced as an "unqualified repudiation of the principle of limited government."[73] Conservatism to Goldwater was much like Aristotle's book *Politics*; it was an "attempt to apply wisdom and experience and revealed truths of the past to the problems of today." Although his "belligerent" style is said to have scared off timid voters, his voice was clear and loud enough to fill the void against liberal dogma that Buckley had identified and lamented. Goldwater is probably most famous for his statement that "extremism in the defense of liberty is no vice; moderation in the pursuit of justice is no virtue."[74] Such hyperbole would do well amongst American conservatives long missing a clear and distinct voice, but it's a long ways away from Aristotle's *Politics*, not to mention his *Ethics*, with their emphases on moderation as a classical virtue that would quickly distinguish Ancients from Moderns.

Goldwater was concerned that conservatives not appear callous or contemptuous of America's less fortunate and that conservatives cared as much as anyone about welfare and poverty issues. But he was equally clear for it to be understood that conservatives should hold these issues away from the federal government; these problems were not to be solved or addressed by the federal government but by the states and their governments and peoples themselves.[75] Along with economic concerns, religion was a crucial issue and problem for Goldwater. During the last month of the campaign, he stopped the showing of a Christian Right film that had been made on his behalf by the "Mothers for a Moral America." This can be viewed in two, ways: Goldwater kept economic conservatism and social conservatism strictly separate, having no desire to participate in social conservatism; and Goldwater both hated and feared the potential power of the Evangelical Right within the Republican Party.[76]

Having campaigned with and supported economic conservatives consistently within the Party, Goldwater was equally consistent in his avoidance of social conservatism. While the new conservatives began to include social issues as a missing link to power, Goldwater wanted nothing to do with social issues. He saw abortion not as a conservative issue but as a question for the courts. He feared that the Christian Right often took away the rights of American citizens. Seeing the potential for social issues to squelch healthy politics, Goldwater held that "equality rightly understood, as our founding fathers understood it, leads to liberty and to the emancipation of creative differences. Wrongly understood, as it has been so tragically in our time, it leads first to conformity and then to despotism."[77] Here Goldwater echoes Tocqueville's early and still increasingly cogent analysis of American democracy.

Regarding progressives and government "handouts," Goldwater said that "my faith in the future rests squarely on the belief that man, if he doesn't first destroy himself, will find new answers in the universe, new technologies, new disciplines, which will contribute to a vastly different and better world in the twenty-first century. . . . To my mind, the single essential element on which all discoveries will be dependent is human freedom."[78] Thus, progress meant better protecting freedom, and the better protection of freedom meant the protection of politics and of differences and struggles for their resolutions and accommodations. That religion is not a political issue is an adamant assertion by Goldwater: "I'm frankly sick and tired of the political preachers across this country telling me as a citizen that if I want to be a moral person, I must believe in 'A,' 'B,' 'C' and 'D.' Just who do they think they are? And from where do they presume to claim the right to dictate their moral beliefs to me? . . . I am warning them today: I will fight them every step of the way if they try to dictate their moral convictions to all Americans in the name of 'conservatism.'"[79] Finally, we see the prophetic insight that Goldwater had regarding this blending of religion and conservatism that he resisted: "Mark my word, if and when these preachers get control of the [Republican] party, and they're sure trying to do so, it's going to be a terrible damn problem. Frankly, these people frighten me. Politics and governing demand compromise. But these Christians believe they are acting in the name of God, so they can't and won't compromise. I know, I've tried to deal with them."[80] As a last statement of his understanding of the importance of politics and of its well-being as dependent upon the separation of the social from the political, we quote Goldwater from a 1994 interview with the Washington Post: "When you say 'radical right' today, I think of these moneymaking ventures by fellows like Pat Robertson and others who are trying to take the Republican Party away from the Republican Party, and make a religious organization out of it. If that ever happens, kiss politics goodbye."[81] Thus we see that if authentic conservatism fails to fulfill its purposes, warding off movement politics and particularly progressive conservatism that tends to stifle authentic conservatism by its similar popular appeal, then we risk the death of politics. That we have almost killed politics several times in our history arises in the chapters that follow. Understanding America's political history helps us understand how the current Republican Party identity crises has ensued and how we can keep politics alive. A revival of authentic conservatism is a necessary bulwark against the constant instability of movement politics, whether progressive or reactionary, and the increasingly greater risks of wandering into the unknown.

Two

The End of History and the Death of Politics

In our own time now, modern technological development has reduced critical thinking in America to group think amongst the populace and its leaders. However, with new discoveries and inventions achieved at an insurmountable rate, people have become easily fooled into believing that we have achieved the apex of human development. Rather than pursuing the greater good and doing as did Ancients in reaching beyond themselves towards transcendent goods, modern societies are content to maintain current trajectories of technological development as fully rational. Moderns use rational processes of judgment as did the Ancients. However, unlike the Ancients, we have made rationality the final judge of truth rather than recognizing it as one of several ways of striving toward knowledge, wisdom, or even absolute truth. As with other Moderns, an absence of deep thought and reflection upon humanity's nature and purposes has reduced the American capacity for achieving political greatness. This is reflected throughout all aspects of both private and public life. In order to fully understand how this came about, we need to know what assumptions Americans act upon and the things that we assume to be correct. One of these assumptions is that correctness equals truth. We believe that when we act correctly, we act truthfully, harmonizing ourselves with absolute truths whether of nature or of God.[82]

Elephants on the Rampage

Directly related to this is the problem stemming from another of our main assumptions— our beliefs in absolute truths carry little weight in our public life. At least, Moderns believe that "absolute truths" should not be valued generally because they are in reality only beliefs, and these beliefs are individually held. We Moderns maintain that political differences should not be resolved by appeals to an individual's pure truth that exists outside themselves or appeals to God, nor should differences be resolved with "truths of tradition." One woman's god does not trump another man's ultimate reality, nor does one man's interpretation of the meaning of the Founding Fathers silence another woman's understanding of the same. We have even gone so far now as to argue against appealing to the original intentions of the Founders, and we decide whether or not we should appeal to these original intentions by appealing to Madison's intent that we not be bound by the Founders' intentions.[83] We cannot agree on any standard of judgment for resolving differences other than our own decision-making. And even in this we remain divided about the process of such judgment, even though we are all agreed that this judgment is the best that we can do. "We" here being a statement of the outcome of our previous decision-making processes or our public decision thus far.

Jacksonian Democracy in the early 1800s may have announced that the "voice of the people is the voice of God," but it is in our current age that this has become a political reality. Correctness is whatever we decide it to be; therefore, truth is ours to decide, to create, and to know. Our progressive ventures into future happiness no longer hold for us any fear of the unknown because we make what is known. We may make adjustments to our projects along the way, but we need not fear awful collateral damage to our decisions because our decisions are truthful and our adjustments are merely clarifications of our original judgments and decisions to embark upon grand projects of perfecting our happiness and the happiness of those around us. Of course, this is part and parcel of modern technology that makes this all possible, including the repairing of any mistakes we may make. Our faith in technology to deliver the goods, even the higher sense of the good itself, is especially unbounded because we believe that technology can be used to solve the problems that we make with technology. We can clean up after ourselves and create substitutes for necessities destroyed, and so on with technology. The people's voice is the voice of God because the people's will can be implemented and perfected. Even when our will is contrary to nature, we can overcome and even change nature, including human nature. With technology, we Moderns truly stand in the place of the gods toward the world.[84]

With such possibilities and with so much at stake in our decisions, the great unknown in our age has become procedure or deciding upon correct and thus true process for deciding upon our decisions—the circularity of the problem is precisely the problem. We try to resolve this final impediment to our wills by worrying over the smallest matters of correct procedure.[85] We now approach decisions about the good in ways akin to managing the economy efficiently or creating and implementing more social and educational programs. In focusing upon processes rather than pursuing greater and more transcendent goals, America has forgotten what the political is and why it is important for it to be maintained. Most citizens are entirely unfamiliar with what being political truly entails.[86]

Rather than using technical means to manage minute details of personal happiness, being truly political involves higher aspirations toward participation in something greater than one's own private life; it involves moving toward duties and rights and relationships within the greater whole of the community.[87] Civic virtue involves the political in that it is an expression of one's pursuits of benefits and the betterment of the political community rather than of one's own selfish and narrow interests.[88] Essentially, the aim of politics is the improvement of humanity's condition in every sense through participation in public life. The conservative element of political society is the remembrance of the community's origins and the roots that have sprung toward particular communal needs and purposes. Conservatives are not innately better than their liberal counterparts, but they provide a necessary role in any balanced political system. If either the liberal progressive or the conservative faction of a political community were to disappear, then such a community loses its political nature and its contest of ideas and methods. Instead, it becomes entirely social and easily polarized in one predominant direction dictated by social concerns and needs, which usually amounts to economics and security as the driving forces of commitment and action. These are selfish, primal drives no higher than those of the animal world.[89] Man as the "political animal" disappears into the second barbarism of highly effective individualism equipped by modern science and technology for selfish pursuits; however, it's poorly equipped for happiness as the end purpose of human life. Acquisition and consumption replace the competition, compromise, and cooperation of political life that draws us out of ourselves and into the sunshine of happiness in a larger world and broader existence of the human soul.[90]

With the fall of the Soviet Union—and this fall's supposed revelation of liberal democracy as the only legitimate form of government or political organization and the legitimacy of its accompanying free markets— we were supposed to have finally reached this happiness for the human family. Political philosopher and policy analyst Francis Fukuyama announced that the world had reached the end of history—the purpose of human beings had been accomplished, and its one political avenue had been proven through the trials of time.[91] However, it's clear that liberal democracy has not triumphed over the globe quite yet. It has not proven itself practically or theoretically as was claimed by Fukuyama. In fact, he merely parroted the more celebrated and difficult thinkers before him: Georg Wilhelm Friedrich Hegel from the nineteenth century and Alexandre Kojeve from the mid-twentieth century.[92] Yes, after the collapse of the Soviet Union, democracy appeared as the only feasibly legitimate form of government, giving liberalism its strongest foothold ever within the global community. In fact since then, "even tyrants felt compelled to call their rule 'democratic'."[93] In the twenty-first century, there are still many obstacles facing the spread of liberalism, yet liberal societies behave as if Francis Fukuyama's claims are correct—that the end of history, while perhaps not quite yet accomplished, seems to be upon us nonetheless. Gone is the age of ideological warfare based on ideas and theories with the potential to spark the fires of global wars focused upon spreading their practices and institutions.

Instead adherents to liberalism expect a continuing and relatively peaceful evolution into global liberal democracy, and something akin to Kant's "perpetual peace" of the future is expected to appear.[94] Ultimately, it may be this type of millennial state that the end of history is meant truly to describe. "For Hegel and Kojeve, 'history,' in the strong sense they attach to the word, refers to the millennial struggle to achieve political modes and orders that secure everyone's recognition as free and equal...there would be no political obstacles left to negate. And hence no more ideas (or ideologies) worth dying or living for. Everyone would be satisfied."[95]

As the Western world continues to make freedom and equality its primary objectives, its citizens have no reason to doubt that mankind is getting closer to achieving the end of history as popularized by Fukuyama's modeling of the idea into a simplified and Americanized version of Kojeve's rather peculiar and controversial expansion of some few implications in Hegel's complex thought.[96] If mankind's ultimate aim is the political achievement of universal equality and freedom, then the peaceful society follows naturally as not only included in that grouping of objectives, but as the truly ultimate aim and good of politics. Thus, the end of history becomes the end of politics, in both meanings of the word "end." However, the accomplishment of Kant's vision of global peace through worldwide equality and freedom cannot be realized practically through politics, meaning that this is not a truly political or universal theory given Kant's argument that what is true in theory must be true in practice.[97] Achieving peace may seem a noble objective, but for politics peace is never sought for the sake of some universal peace but for the sake of a better peace for particular political communities. However, it's an inherently unequal peace for different societies protected by particular politics and political institutions. Wars continue to break out for the sake of a better peace for one or another people, continuing the practical pursuit of unequal standing among nations. It's the stuff of politics rather than of a grand universal society living under a universal liberal state that exists merely for the service of social needs since all political goals—equality, liberty, justice, and peace—are accomplished. While peace may be a social good, its universal accomplishment as some version of the end of history means the end of politics, meaning the end of humanity's striving toward its potential for greatness in the political virtues—the cardinal virtues for the Ancients.[98] Within his framework, the end of man is thought to be social, reducing human beings to living in pleasure, rather than living well, and continually striving toward our true political end, which is happiness. Pleasure, being contentment in peace, is the social good. It's insufficient for the realization of happiness in that it stifles ambition and movement toward the true good, which is realized through life in the virtues, which are political.[99] Politics is necessary to living well and thus to happiness, our true end. Again, "there would be no political obstacles left to negate. And hence no more ideas (or ideologies) worth dying or living for." A world without the political would be one in which individuals could not truly fulfill themselves and become self-actualized beings who are self-sufficient in their happiness.[100] This aim toward the social good is "utopian" precisely because man is the "political animal" and will not be satisfied with everlasting pleasure in some dreamed of perpetual peace. Man will be driven by passions and selfish desires toward happiness instead. Politics will emerge, for better or for worse, from any supposed static situation of peace. The overly simplified reasoning that some suppose from Hegel to argue the inevitability of the end of history is inherently flawed because men are not governed by their reason alone, nor should they be, particularly by this modern rationality that claims preeminence over all forms of thought and knowledge. This modern rationality is logic or logical reasoning as scientific and technological "truth" that is taken as the whole of Truth.[101] While men do improve their conditions over time by observing and correcting mistakes of the past, it is an illusion to think that a full understanding and knowledge of mankind's historical errors and successes will automatically emerge and direct society to an eventual end wherein we will forever remain content with equality, freedom, and peace. It is an ideology. After all, Kojeve was a Marxist, and Hegelian's (and so Fukuyama's) adoption and Americanization of Kojeve's theory is a statement of the practical realization by American liberalism of the end of Kojeve's Marxism, a state wherein politics withers away and happiness prevails as pleasure.[102] But pleasure is not happiness, and a static social life is not the true end of politics. So it is not the end of history even though ideological arguments may persuade us that the world is so, and, in that way, stifle politics as much or as long as is possible but not perpetually. Man remains the "political animal" and must reveal himself as such eventually if we are to escape the illusions of ideology and rise above the fictions and sophistry of modern reason, meaning the illusions of a universal liberal state that is mistaken for the end of politics at the end of history.[103]

We must consider that mankind does currently operate according to a technological imperative by which we constantly pursue and strive to maintain the affairs of society most efficiently. We do this with little or no regard given to politics truly. We give no nod to the life of political virtues—let alone philosophical virtues—or of the good life as the best of lives. Eventually this current type of living collapses in upon itself and society disintegrates because it is not self-sustaining beyond the technical and physical matters of its proper concern. Without any political impulses or forces external to the maintenance of pleasuring peace governing it, society becomes limited in its vision by having put on such blinders in the first place. It becomes selfishly obsessed with itself and with its members, navel-gazing in an increasing narcissism. It's a society akin to Nietzsche's grazing herd living only to chew their own cuds, having lost any sense of higher goods, let alone pursuing them.[104] So, we members of liberal societies should not be seduced by the limited goods of liberal democracy into an entirely forced technical and rational world, even one in which the hope and promise is of perpetual peace and inclusive social welfare at the scale of global 'politics'.

It is part of the role of politics to help a people withstand seduction into pleasure as the good and to resist peace as the highest political good. As people focus solely upon their own social issues, other greater and nobler quests are undermined, and the virtues attached to them and accrued in their pursuit are ignored, renounced, or forgotten.[105] Yes, a modern society can survive and function for a while when sequestered in limited economic realms—facing only maintenance problems and technical issues to be solved, rather than human relations to be resolved—but no society can continue this way for long and certainly not forever. The chimera of perpetual peace is a siren song. Mankind needs to have opposition in all things to find balance. This is the ground from which politics arise, and out of this elevation of our sights are born the virtues that transform human beings into something more and higher than animals.[106] To think that humanity will eventually overcome all conflict is not only absurd, it is beneath the desires of human beings; it is to debase ourselves to life in a city of sows, according to Glaucon's lament in Plato's *Republic,* a city that is quickly rejected in Book II of that masterpiece of political writing. Political life is the platform upon which conflicts emerge. These necessary conflicts create societies and their cohesion in the first instance. Politics is fundamental to human being and to human society.[107] Within politics, we find friend and enemy distinctions emerging, calling for knowledge, cooperation, competition, and conflict directed toward improvement through peace for particular political societies. To rest upon any one accomplished peace as though this is the end of politics, thus the ultimate accomplishment of history, is to then let political life dwindle and suffocate under the deluge of the rising celebration of society alone, without political life and community, as the best of human life. It is to be swallowed up by social interests and concerns to the demise of the human quest for the truly good life.[108] Sadly, the practical reality of this becomes increasingly more likely all the time: "In short (society) depends upon technology for survival and for material well-being. Nations are therefore, so to speak, forced to submit to the 'logic of modern advanced civilization,' which in turn forces them to adopt economic liberalism or capitalism…by and by the 'rational' structures and practices of economic and political liberalism weaken national, religious, and cultural divisions and gradually, but inexorably, economic and political liberalism becomes a worldwide phenomenon."[109]

With this drive to rationally eliminate national, religious, and cultural differences of argument between us, reliance upon guidance external to social phenomena is lost as irrelevant to public life, whether one speaks of philosophical absolutes or divinely inspired truths. Thus, society becomes despotic in its rule of itself according to its own desires and passions unchecked; humanity becomes numb to its own inner humanity. Such social despotism begins as relatively benign. It's a soft despotism that is more overwhelming than the tyranny of the majority spoken of by Tocqueville, in that this more advanced despotism is equipped with and directed by modern technology.[110] Eventually, this must become totalitarian.

Historically, totalitarianism was characterized by forceful control and staggering death tolls. The sheer numbers made the totalitarian state seem successful in its total assertion of power. However, rather than the demonstration of raw power, the truly successful totalitarian society is power made invisible, being administered in subtler and psychological ways. A totalitarian society controls the state with its demands for social goods that are then administered for society technologically. The social goods are dominant in private and public life, totally consuming what once was political dialogue and practice. The social totally consumes itself, persuading, cajoling, and seducing peace across all social differences and arguments, which creates a society not only unified by the state as in fascism, but permeating all parts of society with its object of peace through technical administration through process rather than politics.[111] Procedural justice and procedural "republics" replace justice and republics with their attendant virtues, which are sacrificed on the altar of self-interest as the pursuit of selfish passion, desire, and pleasure. Political virtue is lost as "politics" is reduced to procedure and justice to fairness, and happiness becomes an impossible good. The true end of human being is now mistaken for fleeting pleasures that must be reproduced continually so as to appear to have constancy in its accomplishment.[112]

It is the perfection of this continual oppression of the human soul through pleasure and the satisfaction of desires that now characterize totalitarianism. In fact, this accomplishment always has been the goal of totalitarian societies, and totalitarianism cannot be understood or its accomplishments discerned through simple analyses of its early historical manifestations. Nazi labor camps, Stalin's massacres, architectural demolition, fear and trembling, and all other physical manifestations of totalitarian power demonstrate totalitarianism in the making because imperfect and incomplete totalitarianism relies upon power and violence in place of the socialization of desire and its satisfaction.[113]

True insight, yet to some extent, only a thoroughly mediocre understanding of totalitarianism can and must be gleaned through analyses of the nonmaterial events, people, and places that exist in the ideological world of modern society. Totalitarianism begins to emerge when the values of a given political community begin to change, merging first with social values amidst a people remaining completely unaware of this inception. As citizens gradually become incepted with new ideals replacing their former traditions, a welcoming of these new values occurs as they merge with social passions and desires. Over time it becomes easier, even unnoticeable, for individuals to merge their selfish interests into the realization of a society that devolves from politics and the pursuit of the good into a society dank with group think as social values become universal and homogenous and thoroughly dominant as such.[114] This is modern totalitarianism, often spoken of as soft despotism or benevolent tyranny in order to avoid the stigma associated with its historical origins and evolution. Part of its very success is to be misunderstood in order to misguide understanding and have itself seen as social progress and the advancement of human being to higher states of peace and security as the new supposed "political" goods.[115]

When people willingly sacrifice the essence of their humanity to global peace for all humanity as though it is one large society of equal interests and virtues, politics die as the end of history emerges as an idea of equality and freedom achieved. But again, this accomplishment is one in theory alone and not in practice. Still, the sacrifice for the idea is a practical reality for people convinced to give up freedom for equality as sameness, which is an achievable, if undesirable, fact of this new totalitarianism, which promises the elimination of all conflict.[116]

Liberal societies may no longer be confronted with physical warfare, but as groupthink becomes the norm for their citizens, these human beings must struggle with internal tensions doing battle within their souls. The notion that modern equality as sameness and liberal freedom as the security of rights can coexist perfectly and perpetually is first a farce and then a tragedy.[117] Human beings are by nature diverse and unique. Some imagined global society in which people are perfectly equal because they are forced into sameness, or persuaded into thinking such is their true state, must burst from within according to the expressions of diverse desires, passions, abilities, and powers. Homogeneity is not intrinsically human. Once accomplished politically and then given over to the social, homogeneity must give way to the true heterogeneity of human being. Social powers and institutions cannot contain or "manage" human heterogeneity—that is the task of politics.[118]

Totalitarianism integrates freedom and equality through social institutions and practices, infiltrating and then dominating the state, in place of the state's political guidance. Trying to maintain its supposed perfect accomplishments of coherent homogeneity and freedom, the state must become totalistic in its approach towards maintenance. Equipped with modern technology, the totalistic sensibility becomes totalitarian once fully entrenched within the state and the state within society, so technical maintenance of peace and security becomes the prime imperative of state and society together. All goods and virtues are sacrificed to the hope and promise of peaceful satisfactions of desire, so that a willing citizenry embraces its benign tyranny as society even though the state directs itself toward its own goods of peaceful pleasure without measures or restrictions in any standards beyond itself and its own experience. Current experience and living in the "now" becomes the whole of life, and the celebration of the social system that eventually must implode. The system will crash upon the rocks of inherent human tensions—within individuals themselves and between society and politics—as the political always will remain, however subdued, awaiting its opportunities for expression and action.[119]

Humans will never reach the end of history, nor should they want to, because it means a chimerical end of politics and political conflict, which will be replaced by the social force of mass equality as homogeneity and the protection of liberty defined by a state of social rather than political concerns and ends. Together, these constitute the truly successful and efficient accomplishment of totalitarianism and the legitimization of the totalitarian state.

So where does this drive for the end of history leave Americans at present? Society can be prevented from becoming lured into liberalism's seeming utopia only through a resurgence of conservative ideals and tenets, that is to say a resurgence of politics. Because authentic conservatism is by its very nature a preserving element in society, it strives to hold onto the traditions and hierarchies as well as the conflicts and competitions that are the stuff of politics. The preservation of politics is an intrinsic prevention of any social submergence into global sameness, meaning into the homogeneity of modern totalitarianism.[120] However, a resurgence of conservatism does not mean a reconstitution of the past or the entire demise of liberal ideals. Rather, a conservative revival brings us back to a war of words, reviving debate, conflict, and competition. At its best, this war of words is akin to those of the Lincoln-Douglas debates concerning moral issues and the preservation of social integrity, rather than homogeneity. All this is accomplished through human struggle and talent, through compromise and negotiation. In other words, this balance between differing perspectives is accomplished through politics rather than through technical management of social factions and arguments into homogenous masses. True conservatism is the only avenue to politics in the modern liberal state, and it's the only legitimate alternative to the illusory seduction and mechanical management of the end of history, the end of politics, and the end of human being. True conservatism is the only ground upon which we might stand to judge and harken our pacified society toward the political, and thus, toward salvation from the totalitarian state of technological reason and the tyranny of ourselves against ourselves through the institutionalization of our desires and passions within the modern liberal state.

Three

"The Reagan Revolution"

Many people wonder about the expression "the end of history" or how events could simply stop happening, bringing human history to a screeching halt. But this is not what this expression means. Instead, "the end of history" refers to the accomplishment of the ultimate political goal of human beings through historical progress—the realization of the best regime humanly possible. This is the end of history as in its meaning or purpose and its realization in time. It's the best political arrangement of human beings that can actually be realized and not only imagined. History proves what can be realized—that is to say what is most rational, viable, and true in an ultimate sense of all the organizations of humanity that have been or can be imagined. This best organization is the modern liberal state, most often seen as liberal democracy. All other imagined goals have proven to be either non rational or less rational than the liberal state by their failure to appear in actuality or to endure within history itself.[121]

At the time of Ronald Reagan's election to the presidency of the United States, however, there did exist a seemingly enduring alternative to liberalism, namely communism as it existed in the Soviet Union. The continuing Cold War was a battle of ideas as much as it was a struggle between superpowers. With the rise of the liberal state, "the end of history" existed only in principle so long as alternatives continued to exist as physical realities.

Only with the fall of the Soviet Union could liberal democracy finally be proven as our ultimate political reality in actual existence in time, thus proving liberal democracy to be the ultimate political goal of human reason, meaning "the end of history."[122] President Reagan has been widely credited with causing the fall of the Soviet Union and ending the Cold War, finally disproving communism as a viable alternative to the liberalism of America's Founders. Thus, Ronald Reagan completes in actuality an idea born of philosophers from centuries earlier.

As the right wing *Intercollegiate Review* tells university students, "the Declaration of Independence and the Constitution, taken together, were the work not of a moment, an hour, or even a lifetime, but of two thousand years of Western thought, political struggle, and hard-won knowledge about political power and the pursuit of liberty."[123] Maybe so, but "the end of history" seemed to most Americans to happen fairly quickly as the hallmark of the Reagan presidency, which, when taken as a whole, is seen as the high water mark of movement conservatism and even of the Republican Party itself in the twentieth century. Neoconservative political philosopher and policy analyst Francis Fukuyama celebrated this accomplishment as a singularly American happening, which he described in a famous article followed by a more complete pronouncement in his best-selling book, *The End of History and the Last Man*.[124] His book is a celebration of American accomplishment as much as it is any revelation of history's progress toward its end. Neoconservatives would play no small part in Reagan's contribution to ending the Cold War, and, following Fukuyama's lead, became prominent in the celebration the subsequent politics. These abnormally influential few intellectuals, politicians, and policy makers were part of a diverse, even ironic, coalition that brought Reagan to power in the White House and the Soviet Union to its knees.

The self-acclaimed "Reagan Revolution" signals to us that this is far from authentic conservatism since revolutions are the product of movements for change, and usually radical change at that. Reagan's revolution has even been characterized, somewhat fittingly, as a crusade. Its right-wing coalition captured in the same broad net an increasingly important Christian Right and its politicized morality as well as the secular, intellectual neoconservatives. Reagan finally won the presidency for movement conservatives by assembling this diverse coalition under the umbrella of the Republican Party, a coalition that roughly represented the same wide variety of voters in America who followed suit as Republicans.

The same *Intercollegiate Review*, published by the Intercollegiate Studies Institute labeled Reagan "the most conservative politician ever to have reached national standing in American politics."[125] This publication is a right wing propaganda machine aimed largely at converting undergraduate students to its ideology.—Yet, in publishing this hyperbolic claim, the *Review* followed this assertion with a single sentence paragraph that attached Reagan to movement conservatives by using the word "movement" four times in this one sentence.[126] This was followed by talk of a new type of conservatism in this "movement" as opposed to the traditional conservatism that they also describe. In essence, they do not place Reagan amongst traditional conservatives.[127]

Rather than being authentically conservative, the "Reagan Revolution" and the movement conservatism behind it have been characterized by some as being more akin with the French Revolution than the American Revolution.[128] Presenting themselves as anti-government and liberators of society from the shackles of unwarranted interference, movement conservatives betray major tenets of authentic conservatives—that government and society depend on each other and work together for the maintenance of human well-being. Edmund Burke, an icon of authentic conservatism, wrote that "government is a contrivance of human wisdom to provide for human wants," acting as a restraint upon our passions and their ability to lead us into the anarchy of unrestrained and individualized liberty.[129]

Contrary to such authentically conservative sentiments, Reagan campaigned for the presidency in 1980 on a strong antigovernment platform. Reagan did this despite his previous election to the Governorship of California as a Republican promising to strengthen government there.[130] Attaining power, rather than representing conservative principles, is a mark of this "new conservatism," although only a few among the neoconservative faction of the movement's coalition speak openly of this. Reagan's election as California's Governor signaled the beginning of success for movement conservatism as it worked to claim the conservative label for itself and the Republican Party as its vehicle to national power. The movement had pushed Richard Nixon to work hard to stay ahead of Reagan in national politics and within the Republican Party. But by 1980, Reagan's nomination for the presidency by Republicans, and his ultimate victory that year, finally brought the politics of the conservative movement to national legitimacy and prominence.[131]

Representing himself as the embodiment of America's "good old days," Reagan captured a broad segment of voters by simplifying complex issues for the electorate. He appealed to alienated segments of society, meaning those who were disenchanted by President Lyndon Johnson's spending on the "Great Society," Southern voters who had been handed to him by Goldwater's earlier campaigning, and voters who were turning their backs on the Democrats because of their civil rights policies and legislation and "Johnson's Great Society programs energized Movement Conservatives."[132] A traditionally Democratic stronghold, the South now shifted to the Republican Party and Reagan's talk against the Federal government's intervention into issues that many saw as matters of state politics.[133]

Reagan expanded the coalition of economically and racially disaffected voters previously assembled by the conservative movement to now include many churches and those who would be known forever after as "the Christian Right."[134] Movement conservatives had prodded Jerry Falwell to organize his "Moral Majority" so as to make hay of America's growing Evangelical Christian movement, and they capitalized on Falwell's work in support of Reagan's candidacy. His characterization of events and developments as a "battle between good" and "evil" stimulated the Moral Majority to political action.[135] This was the same morality that Goldwater had so vehemently rejected as oppressive, unwarranted, and unwanted in politics. Republican moderates were forced to give way to policy platforms and candidates of movement conservatives who injected their own version of this good and evil morality supposedly held by "traditional Americans." This emerging group of neoconservative intellectuals and politicians were captured with Reagan's tough talk about communism, the Soviet Union, and his aspirations to end the Cold War.[136] These neoconservatives were an assemblage of Democratic and Republican war hawks who were disgruntled by appeasement and what they saw as American weakness in the face of global communism.[137] The same language of good and evil that appealed to the Christian Right also enhanced Reagan's appeal for these neoconservatives. Labeling the Soviet Union the "Evil Empire" brought Democrats and the neo-conservatives together within the Republican Party and into the embrace of the movement conservatism of the "Reagan Revolution."[138]

According to Jonah Goldberg, author of *Liberal Fascism*—a best-selling book comparable to Fukuyama's *End of History* in American popularity—authentic conservatives had all but given up the ghost as early as 1962 at the latest.[139] He may be right. A prominent early conservative thinker announced then that Americans had already traded their freedom away for the comforts of statism, for what we now call "entitlements." Goldberg tells us that this resulted from the progressivism of modern liberalism and its tendencies towards European-style government. However, Goldberg recognizes that "progressive priesthood brooks no opposition," being "unopposed through our politics, economics, and culture."[140] Progressive politics cannot be resisted, so the Republicans have joined in the movement, creating what we can only call "progressive conservatives" as the mainstream of its party. Authentic conservatives throughout the country and within the Republican Party no longer have a voice and only remain with the party by default, having no viable alternative on the right to represent them in politics and government. These new progressive conservatives pursue "much-needed reforms," but participate themselves in "the real threat, [which] is that the promise of American life will be frittered away for a bag of magic beans called Security."[141] Republican progressives pursue security against "evil" abroad, while Democratic progressives tend to fight domestic "evils" at home. In doing so, both parties accept statism, no matter any rhetoric to the contrary. Each adopts progressivism as the present politics of struggle for versions of a better future according to various plans, blueprints, and experiments of movement politics. "Richard Nixon or (say) Truman and Eisenhower [as] presidents were, in some respects, like LBJ, caretakers of the welfare state, extending the assumptions of the New Deal and the great Society rather than questioning them."[142] Presidents have maintained and deepened the social dominance of politics throughout the twentieth century, building administrations rather than governments. The political values of justice, courage, moderation, and wisdom all have been increasingly redefined in terms of social needs and desires. The administration of the mere life of wants has been perpetuated, driving political practices such as negotiation, compromise, cooperation, and responsibility out of public life more and more. While this has responded to the increasingly democratic desires of the American public, it has at the same time lowered public expectations and approval for politicians and American "politics" generally.

Goldberg sees that Americans try to exempt President Reagan from this sort of administration after the fact: "As for Ronald Reagan, he is enjoying what may be the most remarkable rehabilitation in modern American history."[143] However, this is to admit that something needs to be rehabilitated here, some fault or pattern in Reagan's administration needs revision to celebrate Reagan's iconic place in Republican history. Just what needs to be fixed in Reagan's reputation is his very same progressive conservatism that has been so irresistible to all leaders and reasonably viable candidates for leadership in the latter half of twentieth-century American politics. Somehow, as movement conservatism tries to control the GOP, its movers and shakers claim the label "conservative" for themselves, rhetorically disguising their progressivism at the very least, and also claiming Reagan as their model and hero and as America's greatest conservative. They liken themselves to Reagan while alluring authentic conservatives throughout America into their fold and into their own movement politics.

From the time of Goldwater's rise to national prominence up to Reagan's presidential election, movement conservatives benefitted from the support of large donors who pumped huge amounts of money into think tanks and college programs that centered upon international security and cold war politics.[144] Some of these extreme right wingers, many of them owners of large corporations, were active in The Heritage Foundation, a major one of these think tanks and policy groups. The Heritage Foundation is said to have played a powerful role in overseeing the Reagan administration, being "almost like a shadow government."[145] In 1980, the Foundation provided Reagan's transition team into office with a "blueprint for conservative government," an oxymoronic phrase since true conservatives eschew blueprints, grand projects, and schemes for progress and change by governments.[146] True conservatives are not ideological, but are anti-ideological in their opposition to rational planning and blueprints for government. However, with Reagan, "no private group not officially associated with an incoming President had ever presented such a detailed plan for taking over the reins of government."[147] Throughout Reagan's presidency, The Heritage Foundation continued to provide detailed policy analysis and plans to the Reagan administration and its bureaucratic departments as well.[148]

By the last year of Reagan's presidency, famous historian, political author, and longtime loyal conservative Garry Wills felt compelled to report that "just as Reagan seems incapable of believing anything good about 'government,' he is literally blind to the possibility that businessmen may be anything but high-minded when they lend their services to government."[149] And lend their services to Reagan they did in spades. Besides the contributions of the Heritage Foundation, an enormous number of think tanks and business groups provided unprecedented policy and rhetorical advice, plans, and blueprints to the Reagan administration. Additionally, this advice came with huge amounts of money, which was funneled through many business groups but came from relatively few business sources.[150] Conferences, symposia, studies, and outright personal advice poured in to Reagan in the form of blueprints for governance and change: it was supported by tens of millions, if not hundreds of millions, of dollars.[151] Members of these groups moved in and out of key administration positions—including CIA Director William J. Casey, a founding member of the "conservative" National Strategy Information Center—serving their ideological purposes for both Reagan and their funding sponsors.[152] Movement conservatism was enjoying a high water mark of influence and power that would not be matched again until the administration of George W. Bush.

Their numbers and influence continued to grow throughout the Reagan presidency. One businessman alone funded 110 "ideological organizations" that were "closely linked to the New Right movement." Group after group sprung up with "layer upon layer of seminars, studies, conferences, and interviews" that pushed the "national agenda debate" in their desired direction. Reagan's White House "regularly sent representatives to these meetings...using their leadership as 'talent scouts' for the administration. Reagan nominee Warren Richardson, as Assistant Secretary of Health and Human Services, withdrew from consideration when it was revealed that Richardson had been general counsel of the far right Liberty Lobby from 1969 to 1973.[153] A multiplicity of these groups had alliances with diverse Republican election campaigns and candidates and not only with President Reagan. They intended to change the face of America from top to bottom and from coast to coast. A leader and spokesman central to these multiple groups and activities declared that "we are different from previous generations of conservatives. We are no longer working to preserve the status quo. We are radicals, working to overturn the present power structure of this country."[154] These movement conservatives remained engaged and active in the Republican Party right through both Bush presidencies and continue in the present day.

Reagan's First Inaugural Address is unusual in the amount of policy talk that it contains, sounding much more like a state of the union address than a typical inaugural address. In some places, Reagan sounds anything but conservative. He announces that he is determined to bring down the Soviet Union and defeat communism, not by war, but by "an explosion of ideas and choices."[155] This is the language of ideologues determined that history is a battle of ideas, in Reagan's case an "explosion of ideas," rather than of conservatives who see in history the slow evolution of traditions and customs and of a certain reason embedded within them and the need to conserve these. Reagan's also is the language of progressives looking to move history forward rapidly, again against the conservative grain. In terms of policy talk, his First Inaugural is loaded with economics when Reagan denounces deficits and the practice of living beyond our means as a country. Reagan appeals to large segments of his coalition as he denounces government as the problem facing us rather than being the solution to our problems. Reagan promises responsible budgets, the end of deficits, and smaller government all around. His economic proposals brought in average Americans who had been hard hit by the economic woes of the Carter administration as well as the wealthy few who had the most to gain from these policies. Libertarians took to Reagan's smaller government rhetoric, which went along with these same economics, fleshing out the coalition that had made him victorious.[156]

We have witnessed a dynamic in the United States of liberalism overpowering conservatism by absorbing the American people into supposed political change that tends to be labeled "Progressivism." The appeal of constantly "upgrading" through progressive change has forced both major political parties in America to become progressive. This means that voices of any authentic American conservatism have been dying out, and the tension between liberalism and conservatism is being lost. Without the survival of this tension, instability threatens to ensue as one thought and mode of progressive politics—whether liberal or conservative—becomes predominant. Americans tend to behave as if movement and progress are innately good, automatically discounting the good of any opposing politics. If this were only recent, we might suppose it to result from some subconscious sense of American liberalism as the end of history. But two World Wars created the needs and products of progress for us, and now the ravages of terrorism have made people afraid of what might be unleashed by any political alternatives.

Thus, any authentic conservatism has become discounted generally.

Conservatism is crucial in keeping Aristotle's notion of politics alive in any society. Modern liberalism tends to eliminate politics from society as the epitome of peaceful social life at its supposed end of history. This is what the end of history is supposed to be.[157] This means that traditional social matters are politicized and politics are socialized. In other words, we are consumed by society and its concerns and have left the truly political out of our politics.[158] With this accomplished, conservatism seems to no longer matter to us, becoming as irrelevant as all other political alternatives. Only progress matters now, as we continue to build upon our triumphs.

Any reasonable consideration of the Reagan presidency will reveal that his administration was not as traditionally conservative as many have assumed. In terms of supposed conservative morality and Reagan's promises made to the Christian Coalition, President Reagan proved that he had really only paid lip service to their interests and demands for religious and Christian moral reforms. During his first presidential campaign, Reagan used keywords and phrases in his speeches that would resonate with Christian "conservatives."[159] However, he was later known to be "a notorious cop-out once it came time to deliver" on his promises and policies for the Christian Right.[160] It was not lost on the Christian Coalition that abortion continued unabated in America. Those members of Reagan's electoral coalition who had brought racism along with them as their own form of "conservatism" (again, reactionaries responding to the Civil Rights movement), were more than disappointed with the continuation of Affirmative Action under the Reagan administration.[161] Edmund Burke valued tradition not only for the practical reason embedded within customs over time, but also as the "draperies" of public life that beautify it and comfort us. Once our draperies are faded, or tattered and torn, once our moral values and surer principles of tradition no longer seem relevant to public life and political debate, then political rhetoric must replace them and words must do the work once accomplished by tradition. Hence, Ronald Reagan's rhetorical persuasion was key to his political success, but the revelation of the emptiness of his words left them bare with no drapery left for cover.

Rather than instituting what would have amounted to the reactionary changes that the Christian Coalition wanted, Reagan's gestures for the Christian Right left the coalition more than disappointed.[162] Movement conservatism did not move government policy in the direction of authentic conservatism to any degree in terms of traditional morality. The Christian Coalition responded by expanding its political base and popular appeal to homespun Americans, slowly morphing into the more politically organized Moral Majority.[163] These Christian right-wingers were "infuriated" at the report of a national health study commissioned by President Reagan in which their own "evangelical favorite" and Reagan's Surgeon General, C. Everett Koop, advocated the use of condoms and the expansion of sex education in public schools to combat the spread of AIDS.[164] The Reagan administration was not coming across at all for the Christian Right who objected to these policies on moral grounds. Reagan may have been the master communicator, but rhetoric alone does not conserve waning traditions when it does not translate into public policy and political action.

Significantly, though, Reagan's moral and Christian rhetoric did serve to politicize social matters and socialize political matters—precisely opposite to authentically conservative approaches or intentions for society. Even stepping into the business of school lunches and defining vegetable and fruits for Americans, Reagan denominated ketchup a vegetable in order to satisfy the need for all of the food groups in children's lunches while keeping costs down for school lunch programs. This reach into moral, educational, and social issues, even if only rhetorically, is typical of the modern progressive state of liberal democracy.

This phenomenon, the dominance of material social matters over the political concerns of true conservatism, is exaggerated in Reagan's economic policies and reforms. These were truly progressive experiments lacking any conservative characteristics or merit at all. The economic theory of supply side economics—basically what we call trickle-down economics—came to be known as "Reaganomics," and it is just that—theory. This is precisely the sort of thing that true conservatives avoid, fearing the ramifications of unintended consequences and knowing that theory put into practice always involves myriad contingencies with effects upon real lives. Not only do authentic conservatives avoid blueprints and theories, but they would avoid this precise one and the ways in which it was implemented. In fact, they would avoid it like the plague. The fact that Reagan's people refused to budge on economic policy, that negotiation and compromise were killed as things of the past, showed these movement conservatives digging in ideologically and killing politics. Now as ideologues, movement conservatives' outreach to the public became gradually worse. They now were converting citizens to the Republican Party and not to conservatism.[165] Politics and its key virtues and concerns, stability and justice, no longer mattered to these new "conservatives." Unlike authentic conservatives' emphasis upon these virtues, the new movement conservatism is utilitarian in its use of social issues, using them as tools to arouse anger and mobilize voters.[166] They create vehemence around the issues of "culture wars" to win voters over and to win elections and not to address these issues in governance. They implement their own key concerns of economic policies, making possible their movement toward free-market economies with "privatization, deregulation, and de-unionization" that only end up hurting the very American workers they arouse in anger to enter the "culture wars" as Republican Party supporters.[167]

The new conservatives know that "values matter most" and that they can count on this to rally support for them at voting booths. During election campaigns, they harp on morality and values, but "once conservatives are in office, the only old-fashioned situation they care to revive is an economic regimen of low wages and lax regulations . . . They may talk about Christ, but they walk corporate."[168] Even more cynical was Reagan's use of religion to try to shore up popular support for his policies once it was apparent that his economic theory did not work in practice. The country experienced a recession early in the "Reaganomics" experiment, and the president started meeting with Evangelical leaders in the eyes of the public and purposefully speaking to the American people in ways that began "conflating religion, traditional morality, and capitalism."[169] Denouncing the secular replacement of morality by bureaucracy—a secular bureaucracy that he never deigned to shrink, but grew instead—"he went on to decry abortion, the lack of prayer in schools, and what he insisted was creeping infanticide, and [he] insisted that the majority of Americans who, he said, opposed these trends, must return religion to public life" without ever doing anything about any of these issues himself.[170] He used this language and these issues as tools for popular support, campaigning once again so that he could continue with his economic policies despite the fact that they were not working but were making things worse.

"Reaganomics" came as a blueprint for economic progress out of important business groups and think tanks. David Stockman, a key promoter of "Reaganomics" and ultimately President Reagan's Budget Director, wrote later that the whole "conservative" movement and the "Reagan Revolution" in which he was involved was based upon faith alone, a kind of belief about how the world works, "a kind of a movement"[171]—a loose but precise definition of ideology, the very thing that conservatism originated to oppose. Stockman reports that when reality did not come to match up with these new "conservative" beliefs, when deficits did not disappear and surpluses did not suddenly appear as promised by supply side economic theory, he had work to do. Stockman reports that computer simulations at his Office of Management and Budget revealed that their plans would create budget deficits of up to $116 Billion dollars by 1984. So Stockman reprogrammed the computers to reflect his own and others' beliefs in their economic theory. "None of us really understands what's going on with all these numbers," he said.[172]

This is unbelievably ideological, akin to the scientists in the Soviet Union. They had to make their findings fit Soviet ideology in order to advance their careers on the positive side or risk being put away toward unknown ends if their findings contradicted the prevailing ideology. Good science harmonized with Soviet ideology.[173] In the case of "Reaganomics," however, incentives and disincentives were entirely different and were only selfish either way. This ideological commitment and experimentation is the farthest thing from conservatism that can be found on any ideological spectrum. Daniel Moynihan said of Stockman: "I have never known a man capable of such sustained self-hypnotic ideological fervor."[174] This is the man who became "the voice of the revolution" and implemented "a deliberate strategy of deceit" that he later called "a blueprint for sweeping wrenching change in national economic governance."[175] This is hardly conservatism.

As to the actual working of President Reagan's economic policies, it is a matter of record that his most profoundly supposed "conservative" aspects were never implemented, failed, or were botched entirely. President Reagan raised taxes eleven times, even though he campaigned consistently against raising taxes. Lowering taxes was even a key element of "Reaganomics."[176] Reagan demonized Democrats who wanted to raise taxes and to spend borrowed money, yet Reagan did both despite his paternal lecture in his First Inaugural about a country spending beyond its means.[177] Reagan turned the United States of America into a debtor nation from a creditor nation; he never submitted a balanced budget, and he made huge increases in defense spending that equaled the highest peacetime percentage of GNP spending on military in peacetime ever in history.[178] The American national debt grew at its fastest rate ever in history prior to 200, as Reagan increased the number of federal workers faster than did his predecessor Jimmy Carter.[179] Reagan's growth of the federal government came despite his promise to shrink government because he supposedly believed that big government was the source of all national problems. Ultimately, President Reagan tripled the national debt to $2.7 trillion from the $930 billion that he inherited from President Carter. Carter left with a national debt that was 33 percent of America's GDP, while President Reagan left his "shining city upon a hill" with over 52 percent of its GDP as national debt.[180] Obviously, this spending indicates an active government. It does not appear that many conservative practices were going on during these years, fiscally or otherwise, since the spending indicates a growing actively engaged national government pursuing policies and progress.

This progressive conservative government pursued economic policies with modern "moral" purpose—the reduction of domestic spending should force eventual cuts to social welfare programs and the welfare state, while military spending intended to siphon off those funds and add them to Reagan's dramatic increases in order to combat the "evils" of communism.[181] Having inherited a social welfare state, these new movement conservatives have been described by a prominent traditional conservative as being "stuck with the paradox of holding a philosophy of 'conserving' an actual order it does not want to conserve."[182] Likewise, neoconservative Jeanne Kirkpatrick said that "the Republican Party may not prove an effective institutional channel for the expression of truly conservative politics and should perhaps be abandoned."[183]

Again, Hannah Arendt helps us understand the meaning of this, to appreciate the importance of politics for human beings and the importance of politics for American society. The realm of politics, she argues, originally provided for the highest form of human self-actualization but has since been perverted by our merging of the political with our social lives. Private life and public life used to be practically distinct from one another. The private life of household matters—economics and security—became increasingly generalized for all, enlarged in their public significance as social matters of modern life. Things once approached within private life became public and thus "political," overwhelming us with social matters in place of truly political concerns.[184] Arendt notes that "in the modern world, the two realms indeed constantly flow into each other like waves in the never-resting stream of the life process itself. The disappearance of the gulf that the ancients had to cross daily to transcend the narrow realm of the household and 'rise' into the realm of politics is an essentially modern phenomena."[185] Over time, the actuality of the good life and the truth of what politics are fundamentally about has been lost to us. Liberal democratic society, as a sort of large overwhelming household that has politicized itself, now pursues equality and friendship between its members, finally supposing to be able to achieve these perfectly in modernity through setting humanity's household in order. The politicization of the household, both as society at large and as the smaller family unit, forces the public equality of citizenship into the private realm of the family, its members, and their concerns. This denigrates human beings, rendering a mass of animals living together in society to pursue the necessities and comforts of increasingly sophisticated economics and security. However, without true politics by which we can order and govern ourselves according to higher ideals, humanity will not be elevated.[186]

Without a moral center or stabilizing conservative force to restrain our modern celebration of utopian dreams and progress, liberalism's intended salvation of the social from political conflict overwhelms the social with government administration and progressive planning instead. What passes for "politics" are really alternatives of social administration by the mainstream political parties and social revolution by their extremists and reactionaries. One progressivism or the other have become the only viable electoral alternatives, the only avenues to power. This problem, along with the administrative bickering between the two parties, now counts for "politics" in America. Together, all of this accounts for no more than the administration of Aristotle's "mere life," household matters of economics and security. Over time, society unknowingly ceases to aim for higher goods such as truth, friendship and integrity. True politics are lost to us so long as authentic conservatism remains muted as the critique and viable alternative to movement politics and their lofty dreams of utopian futures.

Not only was President Reagan's progressivism obvious in his economic policies, but it was also self-evident in his equal concerns for national and global security, which were attached to his economics and the goal for ultimate world peace in global liberal democracy. Even if we disregard Reagan's "star wars" initiatives and all the military spending associated with that, we must see an extraordinarily active government working with blueprint planning on pipe dreams as ideologically radical as any communist dream of a classless society. We must see the rest of his enormous military spending as far from conservative, both in amounts spent and in the purposes of the spending. It was only in President Reagan's nomination speech for a second term in 1984 that he even spoke of lowering the American people's "misery index" that was still attributed to government spending.[187] With movement conservatism driving the president's agenda, the Republican Party's so-called "conservative movement" had embraced some new conservative image that included big government and progressivism. The deficit spending of an extremely active government had simply been shifted from domestic policies to security funding. This military spending included funneling government money into the pockets of producers and suppliers of the military industrial complex, a problem that President Eisenhower had warned of in his Farewell Address.[188] Instead of these funds finding their way into projects and policies that directly affected average Americans, government moneys now continued to skew the American economy in other ways, which Americans felt positively only indirectly, if at all. Mostly, the results were negative for average Americans.

This represents a massive amount of money still being injected into the American economy, but it was only entering through different avenues than domestic social spending. This amounted to a mockery of supply side economics, wherein one has faith that the economy will grow simply by lowering taxes and thereby allow more private money to do the job of boosting spending in the marketplace. The introduction of unprecedented amounts of borrowed money (deficits) into the economy to bolster the supposed extra private spending induced by the application of Reagan's economic theory is supply side economics on steroids. However, injecting this government money to wealthy investors and producers in this way, carried no guarantees that these funds would flow freely into the domestic economy, job creation, and so on, as is promised by supply side theory. Rather than merely reducing taxes for the wealthy, government funds were now redirected into the hands of these few investors and producers (who at times produced nothing or nothing of value) instead of toward people who must spend the money immediately for want of daily needs. This sort of "corporate welfare" leaves these trillions of borrowed dollars at the mercy of already wealthy investors and their own "playing" of the economy

This is the equivalent of a gambling house borrowing money to give to the big gamblers in high stakes poker games, who may or may not go all-in, while doing nothing to change the play on the house floor by the thousands of small stakes players who will deliver all back to the house fairly quickly. The choice of government to give funds to corporate America of the military industrial complex, or the few high stakes gamblers, does not force any spending on the house floor by small timers, or average Americans, who would guarantee cash flow throughout the house, or in this case the American economy. Instead, we must wait upon the limited "wise" bets of the professionals for cash to flow, other than a few chips that may be tossed the way of dealers and servers with no certainty what they will do with the "chips" that are supposed to trickle down to the rest of us on the floor. The rest of the chips leave the house in pockets of the winners of the high stakes game or stay with careful players who simply cash in their chips rather than gambling them away. At any rate, they don't circulate back into the ownership of the house. All this happens with money borrowed by the house, money that it ultimately gives away. Obviously, this is no business model; it's a model for bankruptcy by debt. In our case, the house is our government and we are the ones who must pay the debt and suffer the consequences of a bankrupt economy.

In Reagan's case, this was a government that promised to reduce debt and deficits on our behalf then fairly quickly tripled our debt to the tune of three trillion dollars. This is in no way a conservative model of government or economics, but a risky and radical gamble; so it is with the Reagan administration and its theory-driven economic policy. Their original projections showed precisely what would happen, and they simply skewed the numbers by reprogramming computers to make their theory and their projections seem safe and well in the eyes of the American people. The Reagan administration proclaimed themselves to be responsible and conservative, but they had a radically progressive spending agenda and drove us into greater debt than ever before in our history. Yet Republicans continue to celebrate Reagan's presidency as a great conservative model.

Perhaps we have overworked the analogy above, but surely the point is clear: the Reagan administration was a phenomenon of active government, of borrowing and spending, and can in no way be seen as fiscally conservative. From its planning to its adjustments to its unprecedented borrowing and spending, this was a government with a plan. Reagan's economic intervention was ideological and progressive, the antithesis of conservative government.

Like Edmund Burke, Allan Bloom a best-selling author of political philosophy, asserts that "the fabric of community" that is "woven out of certain immediate habits of sentiment" are destroyed by modern reason's aggressive direction of individuals to "see clearly only calculations of private interest. It pierces the veils of sentiment and poses too powerfully the claims of preservation and comfort."[189] In order to counter the social demands upon government for goods and services that ultimately constitute the welfare state, President Reagan tried to appeal to this same self-interest through the sacredness of the free market economy, an appeal that resulted in a lasting legacy of massive national debt that he hoped would prevent government from funding the welfare state any further.[190] This seems to be the only constant marker of the new conservatism that lacked any coherence in its body of ideas at the time. Reagan's massive military spending, despite his election promises for smaller government that spent less, only made sense if spending less meant spending less in support of the welfare state. However, government continued to grow with spending, and the national debt soared throughout the Reagan presidency.

Sara Jarman with Brent Gilchrist, Ph.D.

As early as Reagan's second year in the White House, it began to appear that he would not or could not live up to his election rhetoric. Some "entitlements . . . continued their alarming growth," and government deregulation of business enterprises did not take off either. A sluggish economy that did not respond well to "Reaganomics" combined with a general policy incoherence within the Republican Party failed them at the midterm elections. Reagan's failure to live up to the promises he had made based upon economic theory forced him to ask Americans to be patient and trust him that better times were coming. However, now his administration was the very government that he had promised to get off the backs of the people, but average citizens, at least in part, continued to shoulder the burden of economic mismanagement by the Federal Government.[191]

Supply side economics was supposed to improve everything for everyone, but "something went wrong because something always does go wrong" with modern economics, says the very conservative Harvard professor Harvey Mansfield.[192] This is typical of progressive politics generally when putting theory into practice, especially with economics. The fact that economic theory is not only supposed to improve economies, but also improve people, cuts against the grain of traditional moralists, being implicitly and often explicitly anti-conservative in its claims, hopes, and in its very nature. Yet here we had the man, who was supposed to be the most conservative president ever, intimately intertwining his political fate and faith with this essentially anti-conservative theorizing. He hoped —as progressives do—that prosperity would bring on a brave new world and leave unnoticed his departure from tradition and authentic conservatism. Movement politics, of the left or of the right, renders a multiplicity of errors and vices as virtues when the people are moved by success, by progress. No matter how one framed it, supply side theory was the same old, same old—trickle-down economics—and nothing was trickling. The people had traded one form of government intervention and progressive liberalism for another form of government intervention and progressive conservatism, and it was not paying off.

Four

The Elephants Stir

America's "end of history" actually occurred during the presidency of George H. W. Bush, Ronald Reagan's successor, with the ultimate collapse of the Soviet Union. Bush's was a slow, plodding presidency that matched his leadership style. His popularity peaked with America's victory in the Gulf War, but after the US military beat back Saddam Hussein's Iraqi forces from Kuwait back into Iraq, President Bush refused to invade Iraq to topple Hussein. Bush did so against the wishes and advice of many of his closest advisors and top administrators. They were particularly disappointed, if not alienated, by this interruption of America's transformation into their vision. As a result, it was all downhill from there for Bush's presidency.[193]

Bush was having an increasingly difficult time holding together the winning coalition that had secured the White House for Regan.[194] This was happening for several reasons beyond his decisions at the end of the Gulf War. President Bush further alienated many Republicans, particularly economic "conservatives," by raising taxes contrary to his election campaign promises in 1988. One of his most memorable moments came during the campaign when Bush assertively said, "Read my lips: No new taxes."[195] Nevertheless, he was compelled to reverse himself on this and raised taxes during his presidency in order to deal with deficits and the ever-growing national debt. The

Religious Right also had an increasing awareness that mainstream candidates pandered to them for election victories but repeatedly failed to follow through for issues important to the Religious Right.[196] Other than the dramatic moment of the Gulf War, Bush was increasingly viewed as a placeholder in the White House, a maintenance man for the accomplishments and "conservative" popularity of President Reagan.[197] It is telling that Congress was able to rally enough votes to override all of the many vetoes that President Bush issued between his loss of the 1992 election and the inauguration of his victorious opponent, Bill Clinton.[198] This was not merely typical politics of a lame duck presidency, but it was evidence of Bush's inability to maintain a Republican coalition of "conservatives" with increasingly different stripes. This is evident in the results of Ross Perot's audacious independent candidacy for the presidency after failing to take the Republican nomination away from the incumbent Bush. In the general election, Perot syphoned off 19 percent of the popular vote from President Bush who lost the election with 37 percent of the popular vote against Clinton's 43 percent.[199]

Republicans never accepted Bill Clinton in the White House, seeing him as an interloper. This was especially true for movement conservative, who began to move with a vengeance. Initial efforts to portray Clinton as an illegitimate president included the rising bluster of "conservative" talk radio and, for Rush Limbaugh, television. Full of the same rhetorical bombardments against the sitting president as on the radio, Limbaugh's TV show at the time began each episode with a backdrop picture of the White House wrapped in chains. The graphic was accompanied by a ticker of days that Clinton had been in office and a caption that read "America Under Siege" or held hostage by the Clinton presidency. Conservatives treated Clinton's presidency as if there never had been an election or any sort of democratic process by which Clinton had been planted in the White House by the voice of the American people.[200]

With the presidency lost to them, for the time being at least, the Republican Party's movement conservatives now turned to Congress to assert their power.[201] Newt Gingrich had emerged during the Reagan presidency with a "hard movement conservative line" to lead Republicans into control of Congress for the first time since the early 1950s.[202] Gingrich attacked all opposition as socialist, communist, corrupt, or representing "special interests."[203] He is "famous [for his] description of Democrats as 'the enemy of normal Americans.'"[204] During his administration, President Bush told Gingrich that "you are killing us, you are just killing us" with such extremism.[205] This is what Gingrich wanted, to eliminate moderates such as President Bush from the party. Such moderates became known as RINOs—Republicans In Name Only—and were not welcome in Gingrich's movement conservative vision of a new Republican Party.[206] Opposing several of President Bush's major policy initiatives, these movement conservatives had ultimately "destroyed Bush" with increased griping and complaining within the party, which prompted plummeting popularity ratings for the President throughout the country. Movement conservatives backed Ross Perot's own movement against Bush, creating the end of his presidency. It became apparent that no Republican could win the White House without the support of these increasingly numerous and powerful movement conservatives.

Understanding Gingrich's personal background is crucial to understanding why he espoused and advocated certain policies. Gingrich touts himself as a historian and a history teacher. He taught in a history and geography department of a smaller college in Georgia, working toward tenure in a social studies department.[207] This is typically a six- or seven-year endeavor requiring scholarly publication and at least a reasonably adequate, but not necessarily a good, teaching record. Halfway through his efforts at this, Gingrich switched from teaching history to teaching geography.[208] He failed to acquire tenure teaching either topic, bringing his academic and teaching career to an end.[209] Acquiring tenure requires intense committed effort during a relatively short period of time in one's academic career. During his time, Gingrich not only switched teaching disciplines away from history, he also campaigned twice for Congress and lost both times.[210] His attention to a political career cannot have helped his academic work and certainly must have hurt it a great deal.

These failure along with having earned his PhD in European politics and government, may be why Gingrich gets so much of his American history wrong. For example, during the arduous Constitutional Convention, its delegates reached a moment of crisis and impasse. Gingrich related the famous account of Benjamin Franklin stepping forward and calling upon the delegates to pause and pray to God that they might come to agreement. Gingrich later said that the Convention took Franklin's advice, broke the gridlock, and then proceeded on swiftly to conclude the creation of America's Constitution.[211] However, it is common knowledge that the Convention did not heed Franklin's advice. Instead, they adjourned for the day without prayer. Reconvening in the morning—again, without prayer—they worked through their differences politically through negotiation and compromise, and they continued to work on for some time to eventually arrive at the conclusion of their business and the creation of the U.S. Constitution. Gingrich's knowledge and renditions of American history are scholarly immature and dogmatic, meaning that he holds fast to what he thinks happened and tries to convert listeners to his opinions instead of teaching them knowledge. In Ancient Greece, he would have been known as a Sophist, a teacher of the art of persuasion.

Gingrich's political career also got off to a poor start with two failed attempts to land a seat in Congress. His campaign scheduler for one of these attempts later insisted that "we would have won if we could have kept him out of his office and screwing [a young campaign staffer] on his desk."[212] Gingrich was married at the time to a woman a few years older than himself. This is the same man who later would lead the impeachment effort against President Bill Clinton for wrongs related to sex and a young intern. Gingrich was finally elected to the House of Representatives in 1978, after divorcing his first wife. He served her with divorce papers while she lay in a hospital bed recovering from cancer surgery, and he refused to pay alimony to his wife or child support for his two children.[213] This is the same Newt Gingrich who also would later stress personal responsibility in his political campaigns, speeches, and feature personal responsibility in his "Contract with America." He is reported as having said of his first wife that "she is not pretty enough to be First Lady."[214] Having later married the woman with whom he had been having the affair, he again divorced. His second wife also lay in a hospital bed recovering from major surgery when Representative Gingrich delivered the news with a brief phone call. He had been having an affair with yet another woman, one who was destined to become the third wife of this morals and values preaching "conservative."[215]

Much later, in his 1998 book *Lessons Learned the Hard Way*, Gingrich says that the Democrats had been in power a long time when he was elected to Congress and had no need to change or seek changes.[216] "Republicans on the other hand," he says, "are looking to innovate." We must find new and better ways to do things in and for America, he argues. "We believe we must help American society prepare itself for radical changes" for the future.[217] These are the farthest sentiments from authentic conservatism that one can have. Gingrich goes on to say that Republicans cannot be satisfied with merely stopping liberals; "We need to be proactive, that is, we need new ideas and lots of them. . . We do not need spear carriers of conformity but entrepreneurs of social policy."[218] Again, this is not conservative speech. Entrepreneurs are risk takers, innovators of change. They do not conserve. Gingrich even goes so far as to emphasize this as desirable, comparing Democrats to bureaucrats and his Republicans to brokers on the floor of the stock market, with "a lot of creativity and the capacity to respond quickly to entirely new situations, to break new ground."[219] This is just not conservative in any way. Stockbrokers are speculators and risk takers. This is especially problematic when making the comparison to politicians since stockbrokers speculate and take risks with other peoples' money and trust. This is not a good analogy for representative government of any sort, let alone conservative representation. Authentic conservatives do not take risks, they avoid them and especially avoid politicians who would take risks with the peoples' trust and power. They fear unintended consequences and the possibility that anything gained by innovation might be paid for by far greater losses.

Gingrich believes that his party needs a kind of fermenting or percolating of ideas for the future to emerge. This leads him to favor newer members of Congress who have ideas, he says, over more senior and experienced members without ideas. He even says that he admires the more dissident and younger members, like the ones who tried to oust him from his position as Speaker of the House, because they have guts. "Along with guts comes the ambition to spread one's wings, and that is something I consider essential not only for the Republican Party but for the United States of America."[220] An authentic conservative would be worried here about Icarus and his wings of wax that melted when flying too close to the sun, the unintended consequences of spreading one's wings with new ideas and innovations not tried and true. Such attitudes, if instituted, would have us "crash and burn."

Newt Gingrich claimed to be creating a different kind of political party, something bigger than personalities—a movement.[221] "We are actually a whole new kind of party finding our way into the future."[222] This is a forthright admission that he and his movement conservatives are not conservative at all. He distinguishes his Republican Party from its opposing Democratic caucus by comparing that caucus to a machine forcing all members into conformity. They are a traditional party seeking and keeping power, while Gingrich's Republicans tend to be a party of policy. "Democrats first wish to acquire, and then to use, power. It is not that they have no ideology," Gingrich says, implying that not having an ideology would be a flaw.[223] Conservatism is founded upon being anti-ideological. Authentic conservatives avoid ideologies like plagues for their sore effects. "It is not that they [Democrats] have no ideology," but that they desire power more than they worry about policy.[224] We must presume, then, that when Gingrich prides his Republicans upon being focused upon policy, he means that they are more ideological than the Democrats, which would be to say less conservative than his opposing liberals. Later, he outright says that the GOP cares more about ideology than power, making them less flexible about principles and more dogmatically ideological.[225] This is a problem with movement conservatism. The movement aspect comes to predominate and the conservatism sinks into the background. These are progressive conservatives, as progressive in their own way as progressive liberals are in theirs. Gingrich says conservatives are even more progressive than progressive liberals because these liberals are hemmed in by a traditional party conformity. It is interesting that for this reason, Gingrich says that he welcomes all Democrats who leave their party because of pressures of conformity.[226] After demonizing them and labeling them enemies of all normal Americans, he now congratulates himself for welcoming liberals, believing that he's liberating them to be more progressive within his Republican Party. The ideologies of Gingrich and movement conservatism muddy the political waters. Progressivism and conservatism are becoming less distinct, which means Americans are suffering from a system with fewer checks and balances in the political process.

A major difference that Gingrich sees between Democrats and Republicans is that Democrats are professional politicians while Republican politicians tend to be people who have been successful at other things first and then run for office afterwards to achieve particular goals.[227] Yet, Gingrich's "most obvious example" of what he means and wants as "entrepreneurial leadership in the House" is John Kasich who was elected to the Ohio legislature while still in college. Gingrich also celebrates him as the only Republican to defeat a Democrat incumbent in 1982. Kasich's rise within the Republican party is emblematic of Newt Gingrich's type of Republican and the difference between this type and the career politicians of the Democrats.[228] However, we have a failed university professor in Newt Gingrich, trying to get elected to office twice while failing at both careers. When finally elected, he stayed in office for twenty years, followed by a career as a political speaker, pundit, and political consultant. From grad school, to failing in the academy and politics, to succeeding at politics and making a career of it, that is Newt Gingrich's story, and it's not the story he says exemplifies Republicans in elected office. Kasich, Gingrich's emblematic "most obvious example," does not even get through school before entering politics. Kasich stayed in office for nineteen years, followed by a stint as a political reporter for Fox News. He is currently serving a second term as the Governor of Ohio since the 2010 election, and he explored a run for the presidency in 2016.[229] Despite Gingrich's claims, it's obvious that professional politicians are alive and well within the GOP.

"Why not aspire to build a real Jurassic Park?" Gingrich asks in his book *To Renew America*, stating that "it may not at all be impossible you know."[230] This is about as conservative as his proposal to colonize the moon, which he made with a straight face during the 2012 Republican presidential primaries. Gingrich stood alongside the other GOP hopefuls in the debate, and, despite such talk, he claimed to be the most conservative man on stage. Even if we forgive him for thinking of only the first part of the movie *Jurassic Park* where everything is running smoothly, the rest of story would be enough to cure anybody of creating such things if they stop to consider the possible outcomes, disasters, and unintended consequences, the very bane of their political lives for authentic conservatives. Yet Gingrich laments that "our generation is still seeking its Jules Verne or H. G. Wells" as if science fiction is the proper stuff of political policy.[231] No stripe of progressive goes this far other than Gingrich's progressive conservative icon Ronald Reagan and his "Star Wars" perhaps. Gingrich is not only not conservative in his imagination and political and cultural statements, but he is downright anti-conservative.

While celebrating his supposed accomplishments of "ground breaking change," Newt Gingrich said that these have come about because "there is a new spirit of grassroots inventiveness and activism that is bringing waves of new ideas into the House Republican Conference."[232] He follows this claim with excitement rather than concern with a telling declaration: "I cannot foresee exactly where all this will lead."[233] This precisely would be a lament for moderation and wisdom and slow and careful movement, meaning Gingrich's statement is a lament for any authentic conservative. For progressives, including Gingrich, it is an "onward and upward" call into the unknown. Elsewhere he celebrates the conservative movement's having survived such thinking, having "survived LBJ" and his "Great Society."[234] However, being the man of contradictions that he is, Gingrich also claims that "FDR is probably the greatest President of the twentieth century," words that make true conservatives recoil. [235] That these words would leave the lips of any authentic conservative in America is unimaginably grotesque for any other movement conservative specifically and for Republicans generally. Gingrich celebrates FDR, and by implication the New Deal, immediately after having said that the people and not government can create and find jobs, that American resourcefulness will resolve any employment issues in our time.[236] Gingrich praises FDR for having met the challenge for his generation; "Now it is our turn," he says, presumably to be as progressive in his own "conservative" way as FDR had been in his liberalism.[237] He then provides a list of contemporary "successful examples" of job creation: Amway, Mary Kay, BeautiControl, Tupperware, and a "host of others."[238] It is hard to know if we should laugh or cry when multi-level marketing schemes that leech money from average Americans at the bottom to feed the few at the top are the best "conservative" examples of job creation in America.

In order to foster such innovation and job creation, everything that might inhibit American competitiveness in the world should be reconsidered, according to Gingrich, including government regulation of businesses, taxation, litigation, education, welfare, and the structure of government bureaucracies.[239] In his *To Renew America*, Gingrich provides a plan of eight major changes that must be undertaken simultaneously to address these issues and replace America's welfare state with "an opportunity society."[240] Once again, all major change runs counter to the spirit and sensibility of authentic conservatism, let alone a plan for eight major changes to be undertaken at once. In presenting this plan, Gingrich provides eight brief points with some little description of each.[241] The first two points require but lack significant explanation of how they are to be accomplished. His next three points are merely vague statements of principles. The fifth point of Gingrich's plan runs parallel with and is analogous to the multi-level marketing job creation noted above, and the last three points of his plan involve radical change.[242] The descriptions of these points and of the overall plan provide no explanation nor analysis, and these pages of his book are reminiscent of an undergraduate student's term paper that would be returned with a B minus grade at best for the writer's inability to properly support claims. Meanwhile, "conservative" Gingrich would run with this to dramatically change America.

While building toward the Republican Congressional sweep in the 1994 election, Gingrich asserts that "we recognized that in the world in which we live you can't just have a simple ideology and plan."[243] We are supposed to disregard that having these alone would automatically disqualify them as conservatives while we are told that his Republicans had more.

They had a method, Gingrich explained, of facing problems, finding solutions, and then facing the new problems that came along with these solutions. Gingrich openly names these new problems correctly as "unintended consequences of social action" while ignoring that the avoidance of these is one of the main reasons that true conservatives are conservative in the first place.[244] This method of politics that Gingrich so proudly celebrates is the very method that conservatism was born to oppose; it is the method of modern liberalism. Gingrich believed that he was creating a Republican Party that would attack problems from different angles and with the entrepreneurial spirit that he craves. Again, this led him to nurture those whom he thought could become "important developers of ideas . . . We even need ideas about how to get ideas," he crooned, and then ideas about how to sell these new ideas to the American people.[245] The character of this thinking is ideological in every way, modern and progressive and battled against by authentic conservatives everywhere in the Western world.

Newt Gingrich envisioned himself in a battle of his own on behalf of progressive movement conservatism and its efforts to control the GOP stating, "I am in combat every day."[246] The warrior analogy was apt enough in that Gingrich scared people, according to conservative analyst George Will, and drove American politics to new lows in methods, policies, and concerns.[247] Yet Gingrich proudly speaks of himself and his fellows as part of a "movement," as "conservative activists"[248] — a contradiction in terms if ever there was one. "As activist House Republicans, we were developing what might be called an idea-oriented system"; in other words, an ideology. "We were in the idea business as well as the election business" he said during the take over the House of Representatives in 1994, a House that would be increasingly affected, dominated, and finally shamed by these movement conservatives.[249]

Having swept the 1994 midterm elections, the "Gingrich revolutionaries hit the ground running."[250] These movement conservatives presented their "Contract with America," a document created and mostly written by Gingrich himself. For his help to movement conservatives as they demonized President Clinton with his own radical talk, Rush Limbaugh was made an honorary member of the incoming freshman class in the House of Representatives. Though only one of many talk radio "conservatives," Limbaugh's television show was playing on 225 TV stations by 1994.[251] To accompany their political delivery of the contract to America, Gingrich forwarded the new agenda in his book *Contract with America*.[252] In it, he told the American people that his "revolutionaries" were presenting a "bold agenda that offers up real change" as part of a "movement" for "activist change," continuing their departure from anything resembling authentic conservatism.[253] In fact, the whole notion of a social contract emerged in modern liberalism to overcome the traditionally conservative religious language of a social covenant.

Contract theory was the language of John Locke, the creator of liberalism as an ideology. Locke's *Second Treatise of Government* not only initiated liberal ideology, but it was the first ideological tract in modern history and thus the creation of ideology itself.[254] Modern conservatism was born in reaction to and as a rejection of Locke's ideological tract. Gingrich actually would return to the use of "covenant" while speaking of his own ideological tract, *Contract with America*, proclaiming its purpose to be an articulation of the vision of his new conservative movement.[255] Just as Locke had secured liberalism as an ideology with his tract, Gingrich entrenched for movement conservatism its own status as an ideology in his new contract.

Typical of ideological writing for mass audiences, *Contract with America* lists in point form its key ideas, most of which are restated ideas drawn directly from Locke's liberal document.[256] All of Gingrich's points speak about individual liberties— all but one. This exception is the inclusion of the idea of responsibility, which is reminiscent of the language of "duty" in conservative social covenants. However, Gingrich ends up having nothing to do with citizens' duty owed to the covenant or contract. Instead, it is all about government forcing personally "irresponsible" people to become "responsible" for themselves.[257] George Will says of this and of the Contract with America generally that the "cult of government is finding followers among conservatives." Gingrich's Contract with America, he says, shows an attitude that "Washington should try to shape peoples' behavior, attitudes, and values."[258] The Contract with America is conservative only in the sense of movement conservatism, which is to say that it is progressive.

Newt Gingrich repeatedly spoke of "vision," and "mission," saying Republicans were going to Washington "on a mission." He tells us that his Contract with America is an "effort to accomplish the mission as defined by House Republicans."[259] He attempts to use the contract as "an instrument to help repair a fundamental disconnection between citizens and their elected officials."[260] This instrumental use of symbols, such as contracts and covenants and of language, is generally typical of all modern ideologies, a misuse that authentic conservatives despise and oppose. We properly should see this instrumental use as an attempt to force or persuade, the very method of ideology. This was an attempt to force House Republicans to adhere to a particular version of America — America as envisioned by Newt Gingrich along with his movement conservative followers. The Contract with America is an ideological tract, such tracts being the instrument of persuasion for all political ideologies.

In his *Contract with America,* Gingrich makes much of the rhetorical action of his House members actually signing the contract, symbolizing the binding nature of the signed contracts that abound in the lives of regular Americans. As if actually having made a binding contract here, which he had not, Gingrich celebrates that he has produced a signed written contract that states explicitly, "If we break the contract, throw us out."[261] He expects Americans to believe that this somehow changes things from the normal process and purpose of elections. Rather than Newt Gingrich's contract, the U. S. Constitution is the document that has enabled us to throw Representatives out of the House every two years for more than two hundred years. The Contract with America presumes somehow to improve upon the Constitution and America's normal political process. This may be because Gingrich sees the previous forty years of Democrats controlling the House as a "direct attack on free democratic principles upon which our nation was founded," rather than as victories in elections mandated by the Constitution produced by that very founding.[262] Just as Rush Limbaugh treated President Clinton as though he was not in the White House by popular election, so Gingrich and his "revolutionaries" treat Democrats in the House through twenty-some elections immediately preceding this Republican victory as if they had merely seized power on their own without any appeal to the people or election by them.

The Contract with America is a progressive "return" to a Republican America, not only in the House of Representatives but throughout the country. Gingrich reports that state and local Republican politicians followed suit with their own rhetorical announcements and contracts.[263] In his *Contract with America*, Gingrich announces "dramatic change" for the country. For one thing, he says, the new Republican leadership will apply all laws to Congress as well as citizens. He states this as if the rule of law had never before existed in America.[264] No one is above the law. This is a basic element of the rule of law, much older than America herself. The contract also announces that it will stop violent criminals, as if it could. Number one on the list for doing so is the promise to create effective death penalty provisions, which is ridiculous since the death penalty is a matter of state legislation for most crimes and Congress could only attempt to affect penalties for federal crimes.[265] The "Death Penalty Reform Procedures" announced in the contract have no relevance to states, and they amount to jury tampering by the federal government by attempting to direct juries by federal legislation what to do and what to avoid.[266] Gingrich reveals a certain mistrust here of the jury system and a general mistrust of the American people, who, according to him, need more control and direction by legislation in many respects. The "Mandatory Sentencing for Drug Crimes" has become part of clogging prisons with nonviolent offenders, an unintended consequence that should have been feared by conservatives, and they have failed to solve any drug problem in the United States.[267] "General Habeas Corpus Reform" is promised in the contract, altering the right of American citizens to be heard before judges. Gingrich deems this necessary because of his own misrepresentation of what Habeas Corpus is and does and his proposals threaten our 800-year-old right.[268] Meanwhile, Gingrich pronounces the Contract with America as ambitious, but "only the beginning." There is more to come, we are promised, in this dramatic change for, or rather of, America.[269]

Gingrich's plans in the contract for "economic growth and regulatory reform" and "common sense legal reforms" amounted to nothing more than new tax policies that would benefit the wealthy.[270] Jonah Goldberg characterizes the Contract with America as largely libertarian because of some of its truly reactionary forward to the past hopes and expectations.

Yet, Goldberg says that "Gingrich himself was at the same time proclaiming that his speakership represented the dawn of a new Progressive Era."[271] Progressive conservatism is the accurate characterization of the contract as well of Gingrich and his "revolutionaries."

Ultimately, Gingrich's Contract became a failed attempt to reshape America and Congress both. As its proposals were put forward as legislation, they were watered down by the Senate and, even with that, faced vetoes by President Clinton. "In the end, the inability of Gingrich's revolutionaries to compromise meant they went too far."[272] This represents the failure of an ideologically committed party to engage in politics, to negotiate and compromise rather than remaining dogmatically steadfast. This episode in American government is both an example and an exacerbating cause of the death of politics in America.

The Contract with America marked the beginning of a downward slide of support by much of the Christian Right for Gingrich's Republicans. The contract makes no mention of homosexuality or abortion, two policy matters of major concern to the Christians who helped build the Republican victory and bring about the possibility of such a contract.[273] James Dobson, a Christian leader who had close ties with many Republicans and their individual victories, especially with the younger members, had also played a major role in the Christian conversion and moral reform of several of these Republicans at different times in their lives.[274] To many, Dobson remained a mentor and an influential source of political support and advice. Many of Gingrich's "rising stars" were "more than fervent conservatives" because of their experiences and ongoing relationships with Dobson, who began to take measure of his own influence almost immediately after the 1994 Republican House sweep. Dobson realized by then that Speaker Gingrich really only catered to the Christian Right when he needed them.[275] As well, Majority Leader Dick Armey was seen as very "conservative" on economic matters but not so when it came to morality and legislation.[276] Dobson began to view both of these men as "obstacles, if not enemies." He became committed to getting rid of them and replacing them with his own people.[277]

During the 1996 presidential campaign, Dobson began to step up his efforts to affect the leadership of the Republican Party and to color its policies. Early front runner Colin Powell was too moderate for Dobson's liking. For Dobson, Powell' candidacy represented the demise of the anti-abortion faction of the party. He swiftly moved to intimidate Powell's supporters and tried to silence them.[278] Neo-cons began to throw their support behind Powell, infuriating Dobson with their publications and movement in support of the moderate Powell as the only viable candidate to put up against Clinton. A swell of support for Powell by movement conservatives more than troubled Dobson. These were not his type of movement conservatives, and Powell was not his type of candidate.[279] When Christian Coalition president Ralph Reed appeared on *This Week with David Brinkley*, even he wouldn't condemn the possibility of Powell's run for the White House. This moved Dobson into action against Powell and he managed to stop him.[280]

When the moderate Bob Dole was nominated by the Republican Party for the presidency of the United States, James Dobson and other leaders of the Christian Right harassed Dole for three hours in a meeting before the Republican Nominee stormed out.[281] Dobson bolted from the party with his support. He put his weight behind Howard Phillips, the leader of the US Taxpayers Party, and their policy platform that included executing homosexuals and doctors who performed abortions as well as taking away all civil rights from AIDS patients.[282] When Dole lost to Bill Clinton in the general election, Dobson returned to provoking Republican members of the House of Representatives.

Now Dobson worked all the harder against the Republican Party's leadership. He was especially determined to oust Newt Gingrich from his Speakership of the House. Dobson worked with Tom Delay, a "former sinner" who had overcome his faults and weaknesses through his conversion experience to Christianity with Dobson's help.[283] Both men thought that Gingrich was too timid when engaged in confrontations or avoiding them, and he didn't measure up when it came to dealing with moral issues and standing for the right.[284] Delay would later write that "men with such secrets are not likely to sound a high moral tone at a moment of national crisis."[285]

Ultimately, Dobson would promote two coup attempts by younger Republicans of his own stripe, trying to unseat Gingrich and replace him as Speaker of the House with one of their own ilk. In the first attempt, these "militant" members, according to Gingrich, were willing to join with Democrats in their attempt to get rid of him.[286] Gingrich thought that they would never really do it; They were, and are, very far from stupid people," he later wrote. "They only wanted to cause a big enough stir to get some action on their grievances and thereby bring about a big change in our mode of operation."[287] These younger "militant" Christians wanted movement in a different direction from the House Republicans. These were reactionary movement conservatives of the far right, as opposed to the progressive conservatives at the left of the party represented by Gingrich and his leadership. Reflecting on this first coup attempt, Gingrich readily admits that he underestimated the effort to unseat him. He did not realize how far things had gone. He also recognizes that "most of the Republican members were angry with the leadership for not leading more effectively," but repeatedly refers to the younger members who were actually working toward a coup as "militants."[288] When speaking with the media, he laughed off any talk of the unsettling stirring within his party. Meanwhile, he recognized that the House Republicans were tearing themselves apart. Gingrich would later write that "these militants were so angry that they would even consider splitting the party," as if his being dumped from leadership meant such a dramatic division of the Republican Party.[289] He did report that he "started getting calls from other conservative activist members" of his own kind "to let me know they were behind me."[290] Still, a new Speaker for the Republicans would not split the party as Gingrich maintains, which is evident from subsequent events. Rather, the party was splitting apart under his leadership.

The Dobson Republicans who were "scheming to force Gingrich to resign" aimed to replace him with younger member Steve Largent. They planned to confront Gingrich and demand that he resign or face a vote of non-confidence in the House Republican Conference.[291] They had the support of Dick Armey, one of the top Republicans in the House, until he realized that he was not going to be their choice to replace Gingrich. Armey warned Gingrich, ending the impending coup. Armey would later stand with Gingrich to reassure the House Republican Conference that the blow-by-blow reports carried in the publication *The Hill* were not accurate.[292]

As the 1998 midterm elections approached, Gingrich promoted the impeachment of President Clinton in part as an attempt to unify the Republican Party for the election. Again, Dick Armey stood with Gingrich and gave his full support to the plan.[293] While he led the impeachment campaign against Clinton for behavior related to his sexual "misconduct" with Monica Lewinsky, Gingrich was himself carrying on yet another affair "with a young blonde staffer 23 years his younger who he had arranged to be put on the House payroll."[294] Meanwhile, Dobson worked again to mobilize the Christian Right for another coup attempt, threatening to take his own support and as many people as possible away from the Republicans if they did not meet his "far-reaching demands."[295] Gingrich was able to withstand these internal challenges to his leadership, but his impeachment strategy failed to materialize into electoral victories in 1998. In short, his strategy backfired. The Republicans lost five seats in the House in the "worst midterm election defeat in 64 years for a party that did not control the White House."[296] Gingrich resigned from Congress quickly after the election, not only because his plan failed, but because party leadership learned of Gingrich's affair. He "resigned in disgrace after being reprimanded and fined for ethics violations."[297] Shortly after Gingrich resigned from Congress rather than being publicly dumped by his party, Gingrich left his second wife by phone while "she lay in a hospital bed immobilized after a major medical procedure."[298] Thus ended Gingrich's twenty year career in the House of Representatives, his nineteen-year-marriage to his second wife, and his attempt "to renew America" by legislation.

Bob Livingston of Louisiana replaced Gingrich as acting Speaker of the House. He lasted only one month in the position, choosing to resign the post under threats from *Hustler* magazine publisher and porn magnate Larry Flynt. Flynt had recordings of Livingston engaged in an adulterous affair of his own and threatened to make them public. Livingston buckled under Flynt's threats and resigned.[299] Tom Delay was happy with this, since Livingston had opposed the impeachment of President Clinton. As the Republican Party Whip, Delay brought in the House vote against Clinton the same day that Livingston resigned.[300] With this, Delay became the top Republican power in the House of Representatives, and the dull and Delay compliant Dennis Hastert became Speaker of the House.[301]

Tom Delay was a James Dobson man, having overcome a dark past of his own with the help of the Christian Right leader. Delay's past was full of drunkenness and infidelity to his wife. When Delay entered Congress in 1984, he was a hard-drinking man. Of this time in his life, Delay said, "I would stay out all night drinking till the bars closed. I just did it, and then I got sober and went to work."[302] Eventually, Dobson helped Delay overcome his alcoholism and convert to his style of Christianity. With this conversion came an unusual loyalty and emotional connection felt toward Delay by the Christian Right. They were extremely happy with Delay's new leadership of the Republicans in the House of Representatives.[303]

Delay's nickname among House Republicans was "The Hammer." He imposed party discipline unlike anything that Gingrich had ever done in the House. Delay transformed House Republicans into a "lockstep machine," making them precisely the sort of party that Gingrich had denounced and against which he had so proudly defined the Republicans. This was how the Democrats operated, Gingrich had complained.[304] In his book *Conservatives Without Conscience*, former Nixon White House counsel John Dean writes that "while Gingrich was an autocrat (answering to no one else), he was not dictatorial (imposing his will on others). Dictatorship in the House would not occur until Delay held full sway."[305]

With his development of what was known by his aides as the "K Street Project," for its offices on K Street in Washington, Delay brought powerful lobbying firms there under the control of his Republican machine. Huge amounts of campaign funds were accrued and put to use for Republican victories in their sweeps of the 2002 and 2004 elections.[306] Delay's desire to ensure Republican victories in Texas perpetually led him into an illegal redistricting scheme that would enhance his power and that of House Republicans permanently.[307] In 2002, he solicited campaign funds for Texas Republicans to use in their state campaigns. He also laundered money to them through his own political action committee (PAC).[308] Republicans took over the Texas House with election victories financed by donations that were against the law in Texas.[309] Delay's plans for redistricting would create new Congressional districts in Texas that would eliminate the possibility of Democratic victories afterwards. As this plan emerged in the Texas legislature, fifty-one Democratic members of the Texas legislature bolted from the state and hid out in a motel in Oklahoma to prevent the redistricting legislation from coming to a vote. Delay stepped in and illegally sent the Department of Homeland Security's Air and Marine Interdiction and Coordination Center in Riverside California into action to find these Texas legislators and return them to Texas. The redistricting legislation then was passed, narrowly, and the Republicans acquired five Congressional House seats in the 2004 election.[310]

However, Delay's activities drew the attention of the House Ethics Committee, which was run by his own fellow Republicans. The Committee rebuked Delay for his use of Homeland Security in his accomplishment of redistricting in Texas.[311] Soon afterwards, the same Committee found that Delay was guilty of soliciting funds from a corporation immediately before a bill came to a vote in the House, a bill for which this same corporation had been lobbying.[312] As well, the Ethics Committee disciplined Delay for trying to bribe a Representative to change his vote on a Medicare bill for which he expected a close vote in the House.[313] Soon after this, Joel Hefley, the Republican Chairman of the Ethics Committee, was unceremoniously removed from his position by Speaker Hastert at the direction of Delay. The Chairman was replaced with a "reliable Delay man," and two new Republican members who had sent thousands of dollars into Tom Delay's legal defense fund were added to the committee.[314] Meanwhile, Delay was under attack by a Texas District Attorney who was investigating his campaign finance activities.

In the process of investigating these finance activities, Texas District Attorney Ronnie Earle discovered "one of the largest influence-peddling scandals in American history."[315] Basically the scandal involved Republicans working on behalf of a favored Native American tribe to insulate their casinos against competition from other tribes opening casinos.[316] In his investigation of campaign finances, District Attorney Earle uncovered an unusual donation that "led to a trail of emails disclosing a far flung criminal syndicate operating with impunity at the highest levels of the Republican Party's apparatus."[317] The Christian Right was implicated as well. Leaders had fought against new casinos as "sin" vehicles and lobbied through a "conservative shell organization" for legislation against the casinos while protecting the favored status of the one tribe. They did so under the guise of working to protect "moral fitness" in public life.[318] Jack Abramoff was part of the scandal as a lobbyist who lavished money, gifts, and trips on Republican leaders on behalf of this same tribe. Delay was a special focus and recipient of Abramoff's work and favors. Among a dozen others, Congressman Bob Ney was convicted of crimes related to collusion in Abramoff scams. Delay staffers were hired to work with Abramoff as he, along with high priced Republican lawyers, fleeced Native American tribes of over $85 million.[319]

Although he helped to get Christian Right support for special legislation in support of the unique status of the favored Native American tribe and its casinos, James Dobson managed to remain clean in this scandal by portraying himself as an innocent Christian victim betrayed as he worked for a more moral America in a "battle of good and evil."[320] With the Christian Right still firmly behind him, Dobson put his forces in motion to defend Delay against calls for his resignation and from impending criminal charges emerging from the scandal.[321] It was his connection with the Terri Schiavo case, though, that ultimately would bring down Delay. Schiavo was clinically dead and her husband wanted to stop her life support equipment against the wishes of her parents. The battle between husband and parents ended up in the courts, eventually arriving in federal appeals courts. There, a final petition by Schiavo's parents was rejected by the federal judge in the case.[322] Delay now entered into the battle, posing his support of the parents against the federal courts as a pro-life fight for the right to life. Delay was able to pass a special bill to save Schiavo against the court's decision. He won a two-thirds vote on behalf of the bill in the House, and the Senate approved the bill by an overwhelming voice vote. President George Bush left his ranch in Crawford Texas to return to Washington immediately in order to sign the bill into legislation.[323] However, the law was found to be unconstitutional and rejected by the same appeals court judge who had previously decided the case.[324] Terri Schiavo died.

Having stopped life support for his own father after he was injured in a yard accident, Delay suffered much criticism for his role in the Schiavo case. This hypocrisy was added upon by Delay's law suit against a parts manufacture whose part was involved in his father's accident. Delay had repeatedly railed against trial lawyers and frivolous law suits throughout his life in Congress. Now he was part of one such suit, settling out of court for $250,000.[325] Public opinion came out against Delay and his involvement in the Schiavo case. People thought Delay had exploited the Schiavo's situation for political mileage and had begun to converge into one the Christian Right and the Republican Party in their minds.[326] The approval ratings of Congress dropped to their lowest scores since President Clinton's impeachment.[327] Other Republicans tried to divorce the image of the Party from the Christian Right to change public perceptions that had resulted from Dobson Republicans' actions and specifically those of Tom Delay.[328] Dick Armey complained publicly "where in the hell did this Terri Schiavo thing come from? There's not a conservative, Constitution loving, separation-of-powers guy alive in the world that could have wanted that bill on the floor. That was pure, blatant pandering to James Dobson."[329]

Before the dust had settled from the Schiavo controversy, Christian Right Republicans introduced a bill to try to counter Federal Court judges who they saw as overstepping their bounds. The Constitution Restoration Act was introduced by these "conservatives." It was "one of the most radical pieces of legislation in modern times."[330] In support of the bill, Tom Delay declared that the "judges need to be intimidated."[331] This was an attempt to fight back against "judicial activism." As opposed to "judicial restraint," judicial activism is a bugbear of modern "conservatives." They have a sense that federal judges are making new laws and inventing new rights with their decisions, doing so outside of the confines created for them by the Constitution. When Chief Justice Roberts' nomination to his position on the Supreme Court was ratified by the Senate, he spoke out on behalf of judicial restraint. He said that a judge's role was like that of a referee in sports games. Judges should administer the rules, the law, but not be active participants for one result or another. They should restrain themselves and resist any temptation toward any particular outcome.

However, highly regarded political science and public policy texts, along with politicians, judges, and average citizens, speak of "conservative" courts winning victories in this or that case. They are not speaking of moral victories here. These are political and judicial victories that are supposed to be against judicial activism.[332] This reveals an agenda held and pursued by "conservative" courts, making them just as activist as so-called activist courts of liberal persuasions. Continuing with Justice Roberts' sports analogy, when "conservatives" speak of a court winning a particular victory, it is as though referees can win games just as much as playing teams can be victorious. We maintain that the Supreme Court is often activist, either toward the left or the right, in its decisions. Sometimes "conservative" activism is more obvious than at other times, such as in the case of Gore v. Bush during the 2000 election "hanging chad" fiasco in Florida. In order to stop the recount of votes process in Florida and ensure a Republican victory with George W. Bush in the White House, every "conservative" Justice voted to interfere in the political process. All of these Justices normally are associated with judicial restraint. Yet, in this case, every one of them took on an activist role of interference toward a particular outcome. At the same time, all of the "liberal" Justices, always associated with judicial activism, voted for judicial restraint in this case. They thought that the Court should stay out of the political process and let voters decide the outcome. It is obvious that both "liberal" and "conservative" Courts can be activist in one direction or another.

Judicial restraint is also closely associated by reputation with "strict constructionist" readings of the Constitution, or "constitutionalism," wherein judges are supposed to decide cases strictly according to the wording of the Constitution. Accordingly, they should not read into the words of the document any ideas or implications that are not explicitly stated therein. Judicial activism is supposed to read things into the wording and go beyond what is explicitly stated in the Constitution to create new rights and interpretations out of the document, literally beyond its wording. However, even strict constructionists go beyond the explicit wording of the Constitution as they interpret, rather than merely read, the document. They seek some so-called "original intent" of the Framers of the document, researching their backgrounds, histories, wording in other places to try to clarify what the Founders may have meant in their use of certain words, and so on, in order to aid and justify modern and personal interpretations. It must be noted, however, that these "conservative" judges cherry-pick amongst the Framers for evidence in support of particular interpretations and outcomes. Not only do they pick through the Framers collectively, but they also pick amongst the documents of each particular person amongst the Framers. These judges look for evidence that supports their own particular interpretations and ignore evidence to the contrary. Thus, they see what they want to see in the Constitution just as much as the judicial activists are supposed to do and are accused of doing.[333]

The *Federalist Papers*, a collection of eighteenth century newspaper editorials in support of ratification of the Constitution by voters in New York State, have been used by Supreme Court Justices at an increasing rate as they attempt to interpret the Constitution's wording. Since *Federalist* author James Madison is considered the "Father of the Constitution," these papers seem to be a significant source for understanding his "original intent." However, Alexander Hamilton and John Jay also authored many of these papers. This means that judges must pick between different Framers from within the same set of papers, as though the pseudonym "Publius" that was used at the time as the author of the papers was a single person. In reality, judges using the *Federalist Papers* are picking here, and they're picking mostly between Madison's thought and Hamilton's thought. They also pick between certain papers of each author, choosing this one or that, while ignoring or rejecting other papers by the same author. These judges are looking for support for their own interpretations of the Constitution while ignoring evidence against these interpretations that come out in their decisions.[334]

While many Justices use different Madison writings for their own purposes, they ignore much of Madison's other writings. In particular, "conservative" Justices ignore two important statements by Madison that should guide all judges in their interpretation of the Constitution. First, "conservative" judges as well as their fellow politicians and citizens argue that "activist" liberal judges create new rights out of thin air by reading into the Constitution implications and ideas that they see there but that are not explicitly stated. However, it is a matter of historical record that Madison did not want a bill of rights and worked hard to keep a bill of rights out of the Constitution precisely because he feared that Americans would look at such a bill as a list that limited their rights only to what was stated therein. Madison expected new rights to be discovered and understood, and he expected that a bill of rights would tempt Americans to interpret the Constitution's Bill of Rights as limiting the rights that Americans bear to only those specifically listed in the Bill. Madison accepted a Bill of Rights as a concession and compromise in order to secure ratification of the Constitution. However, his persistent resistance and his reasons for it clearly put Madison on the side of the judicial activists as they discover new rights that are beyond the limited list in the Constitution.[335]

Second, Madison later stated clearly that he did not want nor did he expect future generations to be bound by the understanding and intentions of the eighteenth-century Framers of the document, itself being a creation of compromise and thus an imperfect document. More work remained to be done to complete the American Founding. This was explicitly and repeatedly expressed by many or all of the Constitution's Framers, notably by Madison and reinforced by Jefferson and the other key Founders. Clearly, attempting to limit our understanding of the Constitution to its bare words is fruitless. All judges look to sources to help them interpret these words, meaning that no judge guides himself strictly by the wording of the Constitution, not even the most notorious of the strict constructionists. We should expect new interpretations and understanding of the Constitution to emerge. Though they are condemned for departing from the Constitution, so-called activist judges are in harmony with its Framers and their expectations as they interpret the Constitution. Every judgement by the Supreme Court is an interpretation of the Constitution and not merely an application of its words.[336]

Thus, Delay's "intimidation" of judges to try to stop them from interpreting the Constitution is a fool's errand. The failed Constitution Restoration Act was an attempt to control judges' interpretations of the

Constitution by legislating the bounds of their thinking to attempt to direct consistent and certain outcomes from Court decisions, outcomes created in advance by legislation and not in later circumstances by judgement.[337]

Ultimately, Tom Delay lost the support of his party as criminal charges against him loomed.[338] Trying to rally party support, a "Salute to Delay" dinner only dished up speculation about whether or not Delay would be charged criminally or if he would avoid a prison sentence.[339] Delay announced that "Satan was behind" the attacks against him and the ongoing criminal investigation, as if this would justify his actions and satisfy speculation about his wrongdoing.[340]

Delay's politics were not conservative by any stretch of the imagination. It was progressive right wing politics with grand plans for the future and centering upon gaining and maintaining power. Delay was all about power and victory rather principles, stability, and the public good — the stuff of authentic conservatism. Tom Delay represents some of the most cynical use of party factions ever witnessed in American politics; his use and abuse of the Christian Right (one of his power bases), his corruption and abuse of power, the actions for which he was corrected by the House Ethics Committee, his subsequent interference with the personnel of this committee, and his shady use of campaign funds, all reveal him to be a man of power and not of principle. He was a political mogul on the move, building a Republican Party machine and his own offices to perpetrate grand plans for the future, rather than to safeguard or re-establish lively principles and striving to conserve them in American culture and within American politics. Delay was no conservative.

Eventually, Delay was forced to resign to face criminal charges and a conviction and prison sentence, which was followed by appeals and reversals. He left the House in shame and controversy, and he left the Republicans in conflict about corruption, morality, and hypocrisy.[341] His departure was not much different from his predecessor Newt Gingrich's resignation and exit from the stage of American government.

Meanwhile, Newt Gingrich had been biding his time at a right wing think tank and lobby group, writing articles and making speeches. When it became clear that Delay's ethical transgressions would force him to resign, Gingrich re-entered political life, aiming to take center stage once again. His authorship of *Rediscovering God in America* and his increasing visibility and speechmaking aroused rumors of a Gingrich run for the presidency in 2008. Hoping to restart his political career, Gingrich was busy trying to renew his image rather than to renew America.[342]

The renewal and salvation of American civilization has been a constant theme in Newt Gingrich's public speech from his later years in Congress up to the present time. The Appendix to his *Contract with America* is a speech that Gingrich made to the Washington Research Symposium in Washington D.C. on November 11, 1994.[343] In the speech, Gingrich typically represents his background as that of a history teacher. He claimed he was trying to build upon his background to try to save American Civilization.[344] Gingrich speaks of leadership and the need to learn from the American people, the need to listen to them; "in a rational society, if people know you'll listen to them, learn from them, and try to help them, they want you to lead them."[345] However, this is not leadership. This is ministering to the people, validating the voice of the people. This is populism, not leadership, and it resembles the method used by most dictators in history to gain power through the confidence of the people to whom they then become dictatorial. In this same speech, Gingrich refers to the *Federalist Papers* as the "most powerful single doctrine" that can be used to lead the American people.[346] In doing so, Gingrich tries to make the *Federalist Papers* into a doctrine, being doctrinaire himself, which is to say again the he is ideological and not truly conservative. Additionally, these papers were written by three politicians for the political needs of the day, namely ratifying the new US Constitution in the State of New York. Each paper is authored singly, so even when taken together, these papers do not express one voice, one unified set of ideas. They express three voices combining together to persuade New Yorkers to ratify the Constitution, each voice speaking to different issues and none of them speaking together about any one issue. The two major authors, Alexander Hamilton and James Madison, later ended up as opponents to each other in two different political parties. Along with the papers themselves, history does not support the idea of a unified voice emerging from the *Federalist*. Nor is the *Federalist* a "doctrine" for leadership or any other political matter. What is "doctrine" here is Gingrich's particular interpretation of these papers, which is what he personally sees as the truth of them. The "single doctrine" to which Newt Gingrich refers is his own doctrine. None of this expresses authentic conservatism by any stretch of the imagination.

In his *To Renew America*, we find many of the ideas and themes that will dominate Gingrich's public speech into the present. Gingrich lambastes "university elites," of which he claims to have been one, while lamenting the need for more and better education in America.[347] Again, the man is full of contradictions. He wants America to be remembered "as the center of freedom that, having defeated foreign enemies, found the moral and political courage to revitalize its civilization and lead the human race to even greater levels of freedom, prosperity, and security." This is progressive conservatism. "We are ready for a change of course," laments Gingrich. Almost once a generation, we require "momentous transformation" to set us free again.[348] Gingrich plays upon Thomas Jefferson's statement that every twenty years or so we need a revolution, his famous assertion that "the tree of liberty is watered with the blood of tyrants." For Jefferson, though, history tells us that his own "revolution" was his election to the presidency, implying that the change we need once a generation is the change of political parties as they alternate governing the American people. "Momentous transformation" is anathema to authentic conservatives. Gingrich's "conservatism" is one that goes up against a type of liberal conservatism by acting liberal itself.

As Gingrich promotes his progressive conservative renewal, he tells us that "God helps those who help themselves."[349] He implies that reformers like himself are virtuous, which also implies that authentic conservatives are not virtuous when they resist "momentous transformation." Such resistance truly is the most singular political virtue of authentic conservatives. Gingrich is very strange in this. It seems that even conservatives must be seen as progressive, as anti-establishment, and as part of our liberal heritage. Gingrich announces that we must reassert and renew American civilization, one that he sees as one continuous civilization from 1607 to 1965 and that has been built around a set of commonly accepted legal and cultural principles. He laments our departure from these principles and our unity surrounding them.[350] Gingrich speaks as if we had no Civil War; no mobbing or persecutions of difference of Catholics or Mormons or any other religions; and no persecution of the Irish, Italians, Japanese, and a host of other immigrant groups. To Gingrich, it is as if we had no difference between North and South, no Jim Crow laws, no racism, and no race riots in our history. Gingrich's American history is as unified and doctrinaire as is his interpretation of the *Federalist Papers*. Thus, our civilization is one continuous course of agreement surrounding a single set of principles. Gingrich ignores that America's history is as diverse as its present. To him it seems our present diversity is a departure and decline from the past, thus the need for renewal. However, his plan would not be renewal of the past; it would not be a reactionary return or a conservative preservation. Instead, it would be "momentous transformation" and a departure from the American civilization that he claims to celebrate but wants to radically change. This is progressivism dressed in the clothing of "conservative" rhetoric. Newt Gingrich would be an American sophist extraordinaire were he not so transparent and simple as a person.

Waxing poetic, Gingrich tells us that America must be described in Romantic terms: "To take the romance out of America is to de-Americanize our own country." He asks each person to "immerse yourself in the visionary world of the American experience."[351] This is reminiscent of liberal Richard Rorty's late writing in his short tract *To Achieve Our Country*, in which he asks us to ignore the country that is around us and look instead to our "dream country" for our standards and judgment of ourselves.[352] Gingrich complains that we have gone from the celebration of Abraham Lincoln to the griping and complaining of "present soreheads and jealous losers."[353] Gingrich's "conservatism" ignores the fact that Lincoln was politically radical and progressive, but Gingrich's own progressivism points directly to Lincoln for its justification within the Republican Party. After all, Lincoln was the first Republican president, as we are constantly reminded by Republican references to him for legitimacy for their party and its policies in nearly every regard.

"America is a series of romantic folktales that just happen to be true," Gingrich said; we are unique. Gingrich's progressivism often sounds as liberal as that of his liberal Democrat opponents. Though we "stand on the shoulders of Western European Civilization," we are nevertheless "far more futuristic, more populist, and more inclusive."[354] In his calls for renewal of the American Founding, Gingrich pronounces that "even today this is a very radical idea."[355] Again, we see the "activist," "radical," and "dramatic" celebrated by Gingrich in his words throughout his political career. This is anything but a conservative celebration of American civilization.

It is significant that Gingrich forecasts the great debate of his near future as a contest between individual rights and group rights. "It is a debate that must end decisively in favor of the individual," we are told. "The very concept of group rights contradicts the nature of America."[356] While he may name the debate correctly, Gingrich is off in his prediction of the outcome. For example, when corporations have gained individual rights with the support of Republicans and "conservatives," we must ask ourselves just what a corporation is if not a group? Rights that individuals are endowed with by nature or by God cannot also be assigned to corporations. There are no corporations in nature to receive these rights. Corporations are temporary, conventional creations of human beings rather than eternal natural creatures worthy of America's self-evident truths. At least, that is how a true conservative would approach such a debate. An authentic conservative approaches any debate with tradition and cautious resistance to change, which is unlike the approach of a progressive conservative, such as Newt Gingrich or the movement conservatives with whom he has been happily associated throughout his political career.

Five

Elephants on the Rampage and Rebranding the Republicans

By the time the Soviet Union collapsed, Francis Fukuyama was the Deputy Director of the State Department's Office of Policy Planning. Fukuyama's book, *The End of History* showcased the end of an era—the end of the Cold War, more than it was a guide to the future. His published celebration of America's victory of liberal democracy as the "end of history" was as much a celebration of himself and the neo-conservative version of Western history as it was anything else. Irving Kristol and Jeanne Kirkpatrick had become the most important foreign policy analysts of the older generation of neo-conservatives. Their resistance to any grand plans to remake the world was aligned with the idea that we were at an end of sorts rather than some new beginning. The Cold War was over. American-style liberalism had emerged victorious, and they saw no reason for America to engage in any foreign policy of world domination now. Communism involved a movement to convert the world to a single ideology, American liberalism did not. However, the younger generation of neo-conservatives that was rising to power and influence, Paul Wolfowitz and William Kristol being typical examples, saw things differently. They were convinced that all peoples longed for democracy and that America as the only world superpower was now in a position to help the rest of the world realize their dreams of democratic self-government.[357]

These younger neo-cons continued to gain influence throughout the 1990s. Thus, their predecessors' views of American foreign policy as geared for defense were gradually displaced by a more aggressive interventionist neo-conservative foreign policy of disarming foreign states and of a new doctrine of pre-emptive warfare. Kirkpatrick's reaction to Saddam Hussein's 1990 invasion of Kuwait was that it was none of America's business. While affirming America's need for Kuwaiti oil, Irving Kristol stopped there. He considered any thoughts of invading Iraq and forcing regime change there to be ridiculous. These older neo-cons were realistic about living alongside other powers in the world and recognized that American ideals and interests were not universal. This was not the case for the likes of Dick Cheney, Donald Rumsfeld, and Paul Wolfowitz, however. They pushed hard for America to invade and institute regime change in Iraq during the first Gulf War.[358] This reflects their understanding of the end of the Cold War and the "end of history" as the beginning of a new world order, one dominated if not governed by the United States of America.

The new Defense Planning Guide created during the George H.W. Bush regime passed through the hands of Dick Cheney, Paul Wolfowitz, Richard Perle, and Scooter Libby as it made its way into fully instituted policy. Neo-conservatives colored it through and through. It aimed to keep America the sole dominant power in every region of the world. In this, the Guide was something of a continuation of Cold War policies. However, its determination to keep weapons of mass destruction out of the hands of other nations suggested that the neo-conservative doctrine of pre-emptive war was a departure from earlier Cold War policies. This was motivated by the belief amongst the new generation of neo-cons that democracy could be spread throughout the world, and it bolstered this new generation's determination to interfere aggressively in the spread of democracy.[359]

Early in the 1990s, Karl Rove first encouraged George W. Bush to run for Governor of Texas. Rove redoubled his efforts to get Bush to run in Texas in 1994 after Bush's father lost the presidency in his 1992 re-election bid. From the beginning, Rove had looked upon this as a move toward running for the presidency.[360] After winning the Governorship of Texas, Bush ran for the presidency in 2000. At this time, Rove was known as "Bush's brain" because of the now very close friendship between the two, and "[Rove] got Bush to run as 'a different kind of Republican.'"[361] George W. Bush immediately revealed himself to be a progressive conservative, campaigning on his determination to find a new cause for all Americans beyond daily life. In the years prior to the 2000 election campaign, David Brooks wrote: "[Americans] think of nothing but their narrow self-interest, of their commercial activities. They lose a sense of grand aspiration and noble purpose."[362] Bush promoted "Prosperity with a Purpose" as a prominent slogan of his campaign with the idea of using national wealth as a tool to create a better America. With a sense of personal and national self-celebration, President-elect Bush said in his victory speech at the Republican National Convention that "our opportunities are too great, our lives too short to waste this moment. So tonight, we vow to our nation we will seize this moment of American promise. We will use these good times for great goals."[363] The progressive conservative Bush promised that his presidency would be a "game changer." Such language would continue as characteristic of Bush's campaign and his presidency both as George W. combined the sentiments behind the political rhetoric of twentieth-century populism and progressivism.

When George W. Bush won the presidency in 2000, he had no idea that he had landed himself in the center of what would become a perfect storm. He became the victim of people and circumstances that combined to both take advantage of him and reveal his weaknesses as Chief Executive. (However, President Bush would ultimately respond to these as he learned and grew into his office.) First, the way that Dick Cheney became Bush's vice-presidential running mate enabled Cheney to come into office on his own terms, essentially setting himself up as Co-President with Bush.[364] Secondly, President Bush entered into his office without experience in foreign policy and was relatively ignorant of world affairs. This, along with Bush's religious ideals and sentiments, rendered him susceptible to and dependent upon the neo-conservatives that Dick Cheney carried with him into Bush's administration. Their foreign policy agenda became Bush's foreign policy actions. Finally, the terrorist attacks of September 11, 2001, pushed President Bush away from his own domestic political agenda and moved foreign policy to the forefront of his presidency. This dramatically increased the effects of Cheney's power and the neo-conservatives' influence, particularly throughout President Bush's first term in office.[365]

After Dick Cheney first refused George W. Bush's invitation to become his running mate for the 2000 election, Bush was able to persuade Cheney to head up the search for a suitable running mate. Bush was weak on foreign policy and he knew it. He wanted a strong running mate, someone to help him govern, according to Dick Cheney. While examining a wide-ranging group of potential candidates, Cheney set up the most stringent and comprehensive investigations for his vetting process.[366] For his investigation of business and economic affairs of candidates, he went so far as to request power of attorney over their affairs in order to dig as deeply as possible into their lives. Cheney trusted no one. His standards were unheard of in American politics and virtually set so as to disqualify all contenders. Many withdrew their names from consideration rather than putting themselves through his vetting process. Ultimately, Cheney reported to Bush that he could find no viable candidate.

Throughout this vetting period, Cheney repeatedly told Bush stories of problems between presidents and their vice presidents. The moral of these stories was that the ambition of vice-presidents was the number one problem between them and the presidents they served under, and that anyone who wants the job under Bush has already largely disqualified himself by that very desire. Meanwhile, Cheney kept saying that he did not want the job himself. This and his stories made Dick Cheney increasingly appealing and qualified in Bush's eyes. The more that Cheney repeated his own lack of desire for office, the more Bush wanted him to become his running mate.[367] This placed him into a perfect position to accept a second invitation from Bush, and it was definitely on Cheney's own terms now. Having worked in previous administrations, Cheney had come to view the vice presidency as "a lousy job." Also, Cheney had sought the presidency for himself at an earlier time, but he was quickly put out of the primaries when Bob Dole emerged as the Republican nominee that year. However, Cheney never took his eye off of this highest office however, wanting very much to become President of the United States of America but realizing that he never would be elected as such. Bob Woodward said that this never really extinguished Cheney's political ambitions, and Cheney remained determined to get his hands on the presidency.[368] The closest Cheney would ever come, and he knew it, was attaining the vice presidency under favorable conditions for powerful and meaningful participation in governance with Bush's promise that this would be so. Having served with Cabinets under three presidents, Cheney knew precisely what sort of vice president he did not want to be. Persuaded by Bush's promise of significant participation in governance, especially in foreign policy and defense, Cheney accepted the invitation without submitting himself to any sort of vetting process. He kept his financial information to himself, and whatever background documents he did submit, he did so directly to Bush and to Bush alone. Cheney was thought to add serious experience and "*gravitas*" to Bush's ticket, according to William Rusher, Distinguished Fellow at the Claremont Institute for The Study of Statesmanship and Political Philosophy.[369]

Upon the election of their ticket, Dick Cheney took charge of the new executive's transition team, which was an unprecedented role for vice presidents. While their election was going through the controversial recount and legal procedures in the Florida election fiasco, meaning before their election was confirmed, Cheney left for Washington to start putting together a government for Bush. The eventual president-elect did not get any of his own friends and associates onto his team; instead he was handed a list of Cheney's people to interview for cabinet posts. Even though these appointments were ultimately for Bush to decide, he simply confirmed all of Cheney's choices. Cheney rewarded his former boss from Richard Nixon's presidency, Donald Rumsfeld. Cheney pushed forcefully for Rumsfeld's appointment as Secretary of Defense.[370] Rumsfeld then brought in Paul Wolfowitz, who had worked under Cheney in previous administrations, as his deputy.³⁷¹ Rumsfeld was an aggressive, combative political animal who constantly pushed for more power and turf for himself. In fact, Henry Kissinger said Rumsfeld was the "most ruthless" government official Kissinger had ever met.

Cheney had learned the ropes working under Rumsfeld, which helped Cheney expand his own power and influence under Presidents Nixon and Ford until he became the youngest presidential Chief of Staff in American history. Under President Ford, Cheney said that he and Rumsfeld executed "a pretty serious set of chess moves" as they knocked Nixon men out of Ford's cabinet in what is remembered as "The Halloween Massacre."³⁷² This same pair undermined vice-president Rockefeller at every policy move, and they eliminated Henry Kissinger because he was "soft" on the Soviet Union. Under Ford, Cheney and Rumsfeld became known by their colleagues in the administration as the President's "Praetorian Guard" for their protection of the President and the substantial power that they themselves wielded.³⁷³ In Congress, Representative Cheney had protected President Reagan during the Iran-Contra scandal. Cheney did so after having witnessed and objected to Congressional intrusions into the White House while working for Nixon. As Secretary of Defense for George H. W. Bush, Cheney led the Gulf War coalition against Saddam Hussein's 1990 invasion of Kuwait. Cheney and his people had wanted not only to push Saddam out of Kuwait, but they wanted to invade Iraq and depose Saddam in order to establish a change of regimes there. Ultimately, George H.W. Bush's decided to stop at the Kuwait-Iraq border and not drive Saddam back from his invasion, foiling Cheney's wishes. ³⁷⁴

Now under President George W. Bush, Dick Cheney stacked the Defense Department with his own new brand of neo-conservatives in key positions. Beyond filling Bush's cabinet, Cheney filled slots down three or four levels into the bureaucracy. Ron Suskind said that Bush had no idea how thoroughly overmatched he was by the team that Cheney put together around the President.³⁷⁵ As vice president, Dick Cheney began attending nearly every session of the National Security Council, something that vice presidents had never have done in the history of the Council. Cheney even kept up his presence in these meetings via video conferences while traveling. As part of his deal with Bush in accepting the position, Cheney had gained "walk in rights," and was able to walk into any meeting about anything at any time to weigh in on discussions and decisions, reports David Corn of *The Nation*.[376] Cheney sat in on the President's morning CIA briefings, going so far as to brief himself ahead of time and tell the President's briefers what to emphasize in their meetings with Bush. Cheney started hijacking and controlling President Bush's agenda from the beginning of his presidency by shaping all of the options that would be discussed and proposed in meetings with the President. Cheney wanted control over all important issues that presidents are always are concerned about.

The George W. Bush presidency began as a rather lackluster administration.[377] Little was expected of it, due to questions of its legitimacy stemming from the Florida controversy in the election and Al Gore's having won the popular vote while losing the Electoral College vote because of Florida. During the first week of the fall 2001 at universities across America, political science professors talked to students about the many blasé attitudes the media and citizenry alike held about Bush's future presidency. While Bush had pushed along new policies on education, taxation, stem cell research, and federal funding for religious charities, he was nevertheless seen as accomplishing nothing grand and with little hope of doing so.[378] His chief speech writer, Michael Gerson, said that George W. Bush's first eight months in office "had a quality of randomness, disconnected from larger purposes."[379] Bush was not as ideological as were his underlings; he was more conservative than neo-conservative.

However, Bush's conservatism was progressive domestically; it was based upon schemes for "improvement" and with little regard for unintended consequences. Because of the terrorist events of September 11, 2001, and the subsequent preoccupation of the administration with war and national security, Bush largely abandoned his domestic agenda. We did not see much of it after the first eight months of his presidency, and what we did see was at least in part progressive. Furthermore, everything we did see continued the domination of social concerns over political goods that characterized American "politics" for the past hundred years. This is true not only of President Bush's domestic policies, but also of the overwhelming concern for national security. The securing of biological life, including food, clothing, and shelter; energy supplies and prices; jobs and unemployment rates; social rights and morality; and education preoccupied the attention of American governments and their use of power and influence, none more than the Federal Government and the Bush Administration.

During his first campaign for the presidency, candidate Bush showed his handful of cards on social policies during speeches on domestic and foreign policy both. In a speech before the Council for National Policy, he promised that, if elected, he would appoint only anti-abortion judges to the Federal Courts of Appeal.[380] Education reform and federal funding for faith-based charities were promises made throughout the 2000 campaign. Bush talked about correcting the problem of children living with economic disadvantages. His domestic and social priorities were obvious. In a foreign policy address during the campaign, Bush argued that the military must be used selectively in order to not take resources and attention away from the other "great responsibilities of government."

As president, George W. Bush quickly revealed that he saw education policy as chief among these "great responsibilities of government."[381] He threw his weight behind the No Child Left Behind Act 2001 during the first months of his presidency. In this, he proved himself thoroughly progressive, implementing a blueprint for significant change toward a better society as he saw it. He did so with little regard for unintended consequences and with a heavy-handed intervention of the Federal Government into social policy normally dealt with by the states. He could not force states to comply with his demands for "improvement," but he was able to punish states for non-compliance with the Act by withholding Federal education funds from those who chose to not follow the guidelines in the legislation. These guidelines included standardized testing and teaching based only upon "scientifically based research."[382] Qualitative methods of research, such as case studies and text analysis, were disqualified as "non-scientific methods." These methods have a long history in the development of knowledge and the creation of modern science. They even have an ancient heritage in the origins of science. It is ironic that the administration's claims of success for the No Child Left Behind Act were not supported by the "scientifically based research" methods advocated in the Act. They had to resort to case studies and anecdotal evidence, which were disqualified qualitative research methods according to their policies, in order to describe their claims of progress supposedly caused by the Act.[383] This became an ongoing practice by advocates of the legislation as they worked to legitimize the Act in the face of rising complaints and opposition emerging from the states. There was also a great and growing amount of resistance against the Act amongst educators across the country. Their dissatisfaction with its imposition was widespread and public.[384] The unintended consequences of this blanket implementation of "blueprint" policy included the lowering of standards by teachers as they began teaching to tests only. Programs for gifted students were eliminated as were music and arts education, sports programs, and extra-curricular activities. No incentives were included in the legislation for educators involved in teaching beyond the standards demanded by the Act. Instead, disincentives for non-compliance were implemented. While states were free to set their own standards, there were no provisions for recognition of improvement by once "failing" schools as they "improved" but still remained below the standards required. A significant number of states lowered testing standards and "dumbed down" education in order to meet new measurements of "quality education."[385] Talented students were under-served and education generally became misguided by principles of measurement that signaled what teaching was supposed to be all about. A new national philosophy of teaching reached well beyond the elementary education that was targeted by this legislation, reaching all the way into universities where statistical research and quantitative methods grew in dominance over traditional and qualitative methods of research and teaching. Many disciplines suffered and some were eliminated entirely from curricula throughout all levels of education. The flaws of good intentions so typical of progressive planning went uncorrected by authentic conservative moderation of national education policy. With the absence of significant voice from authentic conservative to balance and moderate movement politics, progressive conservatives continued to mirror liberal progressivism with their own grand plans and blueprints for change in America. Of course, the claims here are based upon case studies and presented according to qualitative methods, so you might dismiss them as "unscientific" if you were educated in whole or in part since January 8, 2002, when the No Child Left Behind Act was implemented. This would be one more unintended consequence of this legislation, since knowledge of these problems is well-known and entrenched throughout the country. Progressive and movement politics dominated the political scene, and while full of good intentions and ideals of progress, these movements ruled unchecked by any authentic conservative force to be reckoned with.

Bush tried to live up to his claims of being a different kind of conservative, "one who is strongly sympathetic to progressive-style intrusions into civil society."[386] However, even with his faith-based initiatives, the Bush presidency more or less maintained the same or similar policies to his predecessors domestically. He stayed the course and changed little, tinkering with tax policies and deregulation reminiscent of the "Reagan Revolution." In maintaining a similar course to the one he inherited, one might say that Bush was close to an authentic conservative in domestic affairs. He managed the household affairs of economics and society just as presidents had done for decades before, the affairs of mere life and not of politics. This, however, would ignore the huge effects that his foreign policy and conduct of international affairs had upon the American domestic scene. Ultimately, "there is nothing truly conservative or traditional about the version of neoliberal political economy that American Presidents from Reagan to Bush have pursued over the last 30 years. Far from conserving traditions or communities or the natural environment, the mindless pursuit of dogma"[387] has unsettled human beings and nature both. If in nothing else, in his foreign policy Bush was a progressive conservative. His political movement in this regard was dramatic, even radical.

The enactment and continuation of the Patriot Act was another area in which the neo-cons' influence would be particularly recognizable. Bush spoke of the Patriot Act as legislation intended merely to fix problems of communication between government agencies and departments. He portrayed the Act as knocking down walls, between security agencies in particular, in order to share vital information. Even upon much later reflection, Bush neglects any recognition of its far-reaching effects upon American citizens, its challenge to civil rights, and its riders (an additional provision added to a bill) that have nothing to do with his stated intention. Members of Congress were able to attach pieces of legislation for their own concerns and not for national security. One of these riders," for example, was the changes made to the sale of cold medicines in pharmacies in order to somewhat control the sale of pseudoephedrine because it is a component in the illegal manufacture of crystal meth (a very domestic problem within some few specific states that has nothing to do with national security or terrorism). In fact, there is a long list of unintended consequences associated with the Patriot Act, and unintended consequences very things that true conservatives fear and are careful to steer clear of by avoiding rash and comprehensive legislation in a single swoop that can change everything for a society.[388]

When candidate George W. Bush said that he intended to use the military selectively so as to not take away "from other great responsibilities," neo-conservative Paul Wolfowitz — Bush's foreign policy advisor — identified these "other responsibilities" to be overthrowing dictators who were developing weapons of mass destruction. By the end of the Clinton administration, Wolfowitz and fellow neo-cons such as Dick Cheney, Donald Rumsfeld, William Kristol, and Scooter Libby, had established the Project for the New American Century to promote world domination by America's super power.[389] Originals of the movement who were more conservative than neo-conservative, such as Jeanne Kirkpatrick, George Will, William Buckley, and Colin Powell, remained outside this new think tank and detached from the emerging influence of the new generation of neo-cons. The neo-cons of the New American Century stripe didn't have much to offer President George W. Bush in terms of advice on domestic politics, but were very influential with him on foreign policy. Bush didn't really have much of a foreign policy agenda of his own; "He truly believes he's on a mission from God. Absolute faith like that overwhelms a need for analysis. The whole thing about faith is to believe things for which there is no empirical evidence," Bruce Bartlett, a domestic policy adviser to Ronald Reagan commented.[390] His personal religious convictions in search of fulfilment set him up perfectly for these neo-cons to use him for their own purposes in the realm of foreign policy and international affairs. President Bush's Christian idealism turned him in the direction of progressive conservatism and movement politics. This predisposed him to be susceptible to the movement conservatism of the neo-cons. They had different motives than did Bush, but they all spoke the same language of good and evil, and together their political actions and policies harmonized well toward active innovation in government and military powers.

Paul Wolfowitz had worked in the Pentagon as part of George H. W. Bush's administration. He and his fellow neo-cons of the first President Bush's administration had wanted more than to push Saddam Hussein out of Kuwait; they wanted to push on into Baghdad and depose Saddam in order to institute a democratic government in Iraq. Disappointed by the decision to stop at the Kuwait-Iraq border, Wolfowitz represented their sentiments in a Defense Planning document that he wrote shortly after the Gulf War. It advocated an American foreign policy that would destroy all other all competition with America's superpower status and ensure American dominance throughout the world. The first President Bush rejected Wolfowitz's plans. However, those in the administration who would later become key figures in George W. Bush's administration adopted his policies warmly. Neo-conservatives Dick Cheney, Donald Rumsfeld, and Richard Perle used the Project for the New American Century to promote Wolfowitz's plans of world domination, plans that emerged as the "Wolfowitz Doctrine." On their way out of power after Bill Clinton's election to the presidency, this became their blueprint for "preventive war," with Cheney and Rumsfeld most concerned with creating an Iraqi ally for America while Wolfowitz dreamed of Iraq as a democratically.[391]

The democratization of Iraq became a passionate cause for Wolfowitz. Together, these neo-cons had been in the thick of Fukuyama's version of "the end of history," and they wanted to be more than observers and underlings in its unfolding. They wanted to make their own mark upon history as it ended in Americanized global democracy.

Islamic and Arab governments were falling like dominoes from the toppling of Saddam Hussein's regime in Iraq, so the US Embassy in Baghdad was designed to serve as the control center directing democratization throughout the Middle East. This was Vietnam's domino theory in reverse. Democracy was moving throughout a large region rather than communism as in the Vietnam, a phenomena that kept America at war there for so long. (The United States has now been at war in Afghanistan longer than it was in Vietnam, longer than any previous war in our history). The Baghdad embassy sprawls across eighty football fields' worth of land. It is "the largest and most expensive [embassy] ever constructed by any country anywhere in the world."[392] This fortress-like center could house over a thousand employees, the number of staff that it would take to realize the neo-conservatives' vision for the entire region.

The Bush administration engaged in grand plans for war and liberation without concern for unintended consequences. There was an expectation that nothing worse could occur than life under the regime they were overthrowing in Iraq, that no unintended consequence could be worse than leaving Hussein's tyranny stand. Thus, there was no plan for what to do after a victory in Iraq.

During the first year of its existence, the Project for the New American Century detailed much of what would later become George W. Bush's foreign policy. Despite the end of the Cold War, these neo-cons promoted increases in defense spending as an urgent need — something that President George W. Bush would promise in his First Inaugural Address. They also revived President Reagan's "Star Wars" idea, something that W. Bush would later include in his defense initiatives while President. The Project for the New American Century pushed for increased American production of weapons of mass destruction and for military intervention in Iraq,

Iran, Syria, and North Korea. These nations would later become part of President George W. Bush's "axis of evil."

In fact, America's invasion of Iraq initially was called by Bush "Operation Infinite Justice."[393] This changed quickly to "Operation Iraqi Freedom" when someone in his administration warned that the first name implied a holy war against Islam. Still, Reagan domestic policy adviser Bruce Bartlett said of Bush and his invasions of the Middle East that "he truly believes he's on a mission from God." Bush's belief is supported by the same belief of his actions by many Christian "conservatives."

In the 2000 election, Bush used his notion of "compassionate conservatism" as an appeal to women and swing voters. Jonah Goldberg tells us that "George W. Bush proudly ran as a different kind of conservative." The Bush team set out to make it clear that they saw the government as an instrument of love — Christian love in particular. The very adjective "compassionate" echoes progressive and liberal denunciations of limited government as cruel, selfish, or social Darwinist, being survival of the fittest.[394] The Bush administration moved billions of dollars of Federal funds away from government programs and into these faith-based initiatives.

During the Bush presidency, the Republican Party enjoyed majority support at the state level in nearly half of the states, with large minorities in the rest, thanks in great part to Christian fundamentalists and evangelists. At the national level, 186 House members and 45 Senators "earned approval ratings of 80 to 100 percent from the three most influential Christian Right advocacy groups."[395] In his election to a second term in 2004, George W. Bush was supported by 78 percent of voters who identified themselves as evangelical Christians (23 percent of all voters).[396] Even though the country was at war and was supposed to be under threat of international terrorism, more voters identified "moral values" as the most important issue of the campaign than those who identified any other single issue.

Much of the Christian Right and many of its leaders blamed "American decadence" for the events of September 11, 2001. On Pat Robertson's 700 Club show, Jerry Falwell said:

The ACLU has got to take a lot of blame for this . . . I really believe that the pagans, and the abortionists, and the feminists, and the gays and lesbians who are actively trying to make that an alternative lifestyle, the ACLU, People for the American Way — all of them who have tried to secularize America — I point the finger in their face and say, "You helped this happen . . . [causing God] to lift the curtain and allow the enemies of America to give us probably what we deserve."[397]

President Bush's adviser on faith-based social services compared the collapse of the World Trade Center to the fall of the Tower of Babel. Yet, when others not allied with the far right asked questions about the culpability of American foreign policy in creating an international environment in which this atrocity was committed, movement conservatives (including Christians) howled with accusations against their patriotism and even against their reason.

Speaking to Bob Woodward while Woodward did research for a book, President Bush said that "there is no doubt in my mind that we're doing the right thing. Not one doubt." The President was asked if he had spoken with his father George H. W. Bush about the war in Iraq. The President responded that "he is the wrong father to appeal to in terms of strength. There is a higher power I appeal to."[398] This is reminiscent of President William McKinley's report of having been on his knees in the White House praying when he heard the voice of God tell him to "educate the Filipinos, and uplift and civilize and Christianize them."[399]

Ultimately, "Bush was persuaded by the arguments, because they coincided with his own Manichean vision of a world divided between the forces of good and evil."[400]

Through his many unilateral policy decisions, Bush more than doubled the national debt that he inherited. This was largely due to massive military expenditures while simultaneously cutting taxes for America's wealthiest few. The disparity between rich and poor in the United States became greater than ever. Regarding similar disparities of an earlier age, Supreme Court

Justice Louis Brandeis said that "we can have democracy in this country, or we can have great wealth concentrated in the hands of a few, but we can't have both."[401] Ironically, or cynically perhaps, the Bush administration was debasing democracy at home while on its quixotic venture to spread democracy abroad in the Middle East.

Bush's international activism drove American debt into the hands of foreigners, setting the United States up for potential instability at the mercy of other sovereign powers and foreign private investors if they ever should stop lending us money or simply call in the debt. During Bush's first term as president, Vice President Dick Cheney "publicly informed the Secretary of the Treasury that 'deficits don't matter.'"[402] By the end of this first term in 2004, the country was in its worst recession since the years of the Great Depression. President Bush "received the highest disapproval rating, 71 percent, since the Gallup Poll began its surveys in the 1930s."[403] Nevertheless, he prevailed in his election to a second term in office.

By 2008, people around the world had come to see the United States as the "country that stands out as a negative force in the world."[404] Even 52 percent of Canadians, America's longtime best friend and trading partner, declared that this was so, and only 21 percent named Iran as a distant second. Meanwhile on the home front, soon after the end of Bush's presidency, frustrated Republicans began questioning the general direction and true motivation of the GOP establishment. What started as gradual rumblings among angsty conservative voters soon erupted full force, and the Tea Party was born.

The Tea Party movement emerged in 2009 as an expression of activist "conservative" anger, especially that of younger politicians and GOP movement conservatives. This represents a reactionary move farther to the right of the Party than any other faction. While libertarians in the party are far right reactionaries, wanting to return to the economics and liberties of America's "golden age" of the Founding era, Tea Partiers combine this with a reactionary moral element as well. There is an overlap here with the Christian Right and the remnants of the Christian Coalition, which means the Tea Party began as an extremely loose coalition of diverse reactionary "conservatives." Many were focused on taxes, deficits, and economic policies of the Federal government while others were largely religious in their motivations. Still others combined elements of both concerns. Essentially, this was a diverse grassroots movement beginning without any specific leadership or coherent policy platform. Many in the Tea Party never understood the implication of the party's name. They had many concerns and did not realize that their name implied a clear and singular focus on taxes, as in the original Boston Tea Party. Still, there was enough coherence in the movement to pressure Republican candidates to cater to them and espouse reactionary movement conservative policies in order to secure Tea Party support. The Republicans swept the 2010 midterm election with eighty-seven freshmen elected largely because of Tea Party support.[405]

Tea Party complaints have been likened to the sympathies of the Anti-Federalists against the ratification of the Constitution. Anti-Federalists feared a large, powerful central government, the office of the presidency, and the removal of political influence from the people. The "party" also took issue with the new residency with elite representatives because they removed popular opinion in a large extended republic. "The Anti-Federalists lost the battle over the ratification of the Constitution, but they continue to be an animating force in American politics . . . most recently in the Tea Party-powered takeover of the House in 2010."[406] This return to pre-Constitutional ideals is anything but conservative. It is a reactionary movement that hearkens back to ideals and arguments defeated hundreds of years ago, but Tea Party sentiments see their ideology as a new romantic Americanism of longing for the past. This sort of movement is as radical and revolutionary as any political ideology of the far left with potency for upheaval and chaos should it ever prevail.

Echoing similar sentiments, George W. Bush speechwriter Michael Gerson's August 2010 *Washington Post* column "Why the Tea Party Is Toxic for the GOP," argued against the movement's view of the Constitution as well as its general disconnection from prevailing sentiments and other factions within the Republican Party. "Tea Party populism is . . . clearly incompatible with some conservative and Republican beliefs. It is at odds with Abraham Lincoln's inclusive tone and his conviction that government policies could empower individuals. It is inconsistent with religious teaching on government's responsibility to seek the common good and to care for the weak. It does not reflect a Burkean suspicion of radical social change," Gerson wrote.[407] While this certainly is correct, the same may be said of movement conservatism and the other more vocal factions within the Republican Party.

Tea Party "populists" are of a different sort than those of earlier American populist movements. Those movements engaged farmers, laborers, and "rural folk" in contests against the interests of capitalism and city dwellers as American urbanization progressed in an almost revolutionary manner akin to the industrial revolution or the more recent technology and information revolutions. Tea Partiers tend to be educated white middle class office workers and city dwellers who embrace capitalism wholeheartedly.

Despite the sense of some that Tea Party support is declining, according to an October 2014 Gallup Poll, 24 percent of Americans continue to support the movement.[408] While Gallup notes that support for the Tea Party is down since 2010, support has actually "been fairly stable since late 2011."[409] Twenty-eight percent of Tea Party Republicans classify themselves as very conservative, and 49 percent classify themselves as conservative.[410] Tea Partiers associate themselves and their movement with the inherent tenants of conservatism. Given that Tea Partiers have paired conservative and Tea Party values together (as noted in the correlation between individuals who both support the Tea Party and those who identify as both "very conservative" and "conservative"), elected officials cannot ignore the movement. Hence, Tea Partiers continue to have a significant impact on Congressional politics and have proven able to oust longtime incumbents from office whether Republican or Democrat. Tea Party candidates have been able to circumvent the Republican National Committee in primary elections to win GOP nominations in general elections. Private donors and organizers have provided members of the Tea Party with enough independence from the Republican Party machine to be able to challenge it and its favored incumbents and candidates. GOP leadership laments that Tea

Partiers are thus enabled to win nominations in the primary process, but they are "ideological extremists" who cannot carry the day in general elections, thus losing Republican seats in Congress.

While Tea Partiers are as likely to care about state and local issues as much as national ones, they still conduct an openly rebellious and cantankerous movement within the national Republican Party. They are "activists" who persistently denounce "RINOS" (Republicans in Name Only), but at the same time they are suspicious of the power of the Republican Party and its ability to coerce conformity. Thus, the Tea Party remains an insurgent movement rather than a controlling organization within the Republican Party, and it prevails ideologically over other factions within the party even if they lose election contests to those factions. However, in late 2013, Jonah Goldberg asserted that it is authentic conservatives who really are "RINOS" because the Republican Party has become so altered from the past and is now so entirely movement and future-oriented that "conservative purists" no longer fit as truly Republican. It is the rest of the party — the zealots, extremists, and progressives — that truly represent the GOP now rather than conservatives. If true conservatives are now characterized as "Republican in Name Only," the implication is that authentic Republicans who are the voices and faces of the party now must be seen as "Conservative in Name Only."

Due to some of the brand damage that the Tea Party rendered to the Republican Party, several campaigns have emerged in recent years to alter the nation's perceptions of the party. However, while Republicans have gone through several re-branding and redefining ventures over the decades — as illustrated in earlier chapters — the most recent approach is proving to be more harmful than not. This damage has been wrought by the reactionary attitudes of Tea Party members and from conservatives who have begun to pander to progressive ideals. In an article by *The Associated Press* in 2012, the writer noted that, "[Obama's] Republican rivals are forced to keep emphasizing their conservative credentials to attract the right-leaning activists who dominate the nominating contests."[411] These "right-leaning activist" Tea Partiers are not only dangerous for the superficial image of the Republican Party, but they also undermine traditionally conservative principles. In fact, while Tea Partiers espouse government reform through adopting libertarian and conservative principles, they actually use tactics similar to progressives in accomplishing their goals. When supposed conservatives use the movement tactics of progressives to accomplish their aims, qualities such as patience, temperance, and moderation, for which conservatives are known dissipate from society.

Without the balancing force that conservatism provides against the driving force of modern progressivism, the political system becomes more susceptible to destabilization. For example, Ryan Hecker, a key Tea Party leader, led efforts to create and organize a contract entitled, *Contract from America*.[412] Creating a document that congressional candidates should abide by seems more reminiscent of a progressive or programmatic tactic rather than of a libertarian or conservative approach. Some of the charges issued by the contract include, "identify constitutionality of every new law" and "audit federal government agencies for constitutionality." A true libertarian or conservative believes no one should be told how to think, so they might balk at the contract's claims, claims that would create a more burdensome regime rather than aid toward developing a political perspective. Because these types of tactics have slowly infused themselves into the Republican Party, members are more unaware than not of their own party's devolution into more revolutionary tactics.

The Republican Party's adherence to its own conservative value system has come into question. A significant number of individuals within the party, whether they are constituents or the leaders themselves, have succumbed to either becoming more reactionary or progressive in their conservatism. And if they themselves are not reactionary or progressive in nature, Republican leaders still feel compelled to cater to the needs of Tea Partiers given their majority. In a number of situations, former Republicans have simply started to register as Independent voters or joined other third party alternatives. Around 40 to 45 percent of Americans identify themselves as being independent, according to a 2014 Gallup Poll.[413] Voter enrollment on both Republican and Democrat sides is down because many independents "are ashamed to be associated with either party," Dr. Christopher Karpowitz, Co-Director of the BYU Center for the Study of Elections and Democracy noted.[414] However, according to a November 2014 article in the Washington Post, most of these Independents are primarily disaffected conservatives. In discussing why Republicans swept the 2014 midterm elections, writers Samara Klar and Yanna Krupnikov concluded, "Why did these alleged swing voters swing right? It is because independents who voted for Republicans were simply Republicans all along." And, according to Klar and Krupnikov, "Independents — by and large — are partisans gone undercover. Why? Because the label "independent" conveys a more positive image, and most people want to convey the best image possible."[415]

A significant number of conservative voters are either distancing themselves from the party or have become swept up in more movement-based aspects, especially given the lack of unification amongst Republican leadership. One example of this fractiousness is illustrated between former Speaker of the House John A. Boehner who constantly tried to downplay Republican divisiveness, and the more reactionary Tea Partier Rep. Louie Gohmert who campaigned to replace Boehner in early 2015. These two men campaign under the same party name, yet their public statements place them on diametrically opposed sides of the Republican ideological spectrum even though both say they adhere to "conservative" ideals. Truly conservative ideals, such as those seen in the likes of Russell Kirk and William Buckley, seem to be a rare breed now. This is a troubling notion because many, especially the younger generation, are unaware of just how far their own conservatism has become distanced from its original roots. If Republicans are unaware of how far they have strayed in the first place, then it becomes that much harder to move back on course. They cannot find a solution if they are unable to articulately define and perceive the problem themselves.

Yet, for all the rallies and phones calls made by Tea Partiers to congressional offices, and for all the speeches given by former US House Representative Michele Bachmann (who chaired the first Tea Party caucus in 2010) and Senators Mike Lee and Ted Cruz about the necessary reinsurgence of conservative values within society, many rank-and-file members of the Republican Party sense something awry in their tactics. Their revival of conservatism does not use conservative methods. The Tea Party's emergence was almost like a mass gut reaction in response to Democrats landslide victories in previous elections and to the growing confusion within the party left by the Bush administration's legacy. This reactionary movement is proving to be more harmful than not for the long-term health and cause of the Republican Party.

Former Republican Governor of Florida Charlie Crist, after having crossed over to the Democrats, complained that the "Extreme Right" has "hijacked the GOP."[416] Crist characterized the party as "brimming with Tea Party fervor and anti-Obama zeal" by the time of the 2012 Republican National Convention. Speaking at the Democratic National Convention, Crist began his speech by stating that "half a century ago, Ronald Reagan, the man whose optimism inspired me to enter politics, famously said that he didn't leave the Democratic Party, but the party left him. Well, listen," Crist continued, "I can relate. I didn't leave the Republican Party. It left me." Crist went on to say "my friend Jeb Bush recently noted Reagan himself would have been too moderate, too reasonable for today's GOP." This is how Crist found himself to be a moderate without a home in the Republican Party. Crist was happy to find a new home among the Democrats with whom conformity was not coerced or enforced, he maintained, unlike the twenty-first century Republican Party that he characterized as oppressively binding members to checklists of policy issues and enforcing no negotiation and no compromise "politics."[417] The world had turned upside down since Newt Gingrich's description and celebration of the two parties' differences. A somersault that began immediately upon Gingrich's resignation from Congress now continued turning to the extreme. The factions that now influence, if not control, Republican Party policies and members' actions "are allergic to the very idea of compromise," which is to say they are allergic to politics. "Crazy extremists hijacked the party," according to Crist, and "drove it off an ideological cliff."[418]

Sara Jarman with Brent Gilchrist, Ph.D.

Conservatives are and were having a difficult time trying to define themselves against constantly rising tides of progressive ideals, but because of the schisms that the Tea Party has created within the party, Republicans now are waging multiple battles on several fronts. In democratic politics as in war deploying your troops onto multiple fronts sows inevitable defeat. Republicans need to pick a battle to fight rather than entrench themselves in both a domestic struggle within their own party and in a foreign one against the Democrats. After all, a house divided against itself cannot stand. Republicans need to pause to ask the essential questions: "Who are we, what are our defining principles, and how do our goals reflect those principles? To accomplish these goals, are we guilty of using the same tactics and playbook as the left, falling back on the adage that the ends justify the means?" Without performing a necessary reassessment of their identity and facing the overwhelming influence of progressive and movement politics, Republicans can only exacerbate the inevitable unraveling of any conservative influence within the American polity.

In order to garner greater support amongst the American populace, Republicans need to market their cause and perhaps rebrand their message. Branding a product is a superficial enterprise, but if done right can actually provide the necessary in-depth overhaul for ensuring a causes' lasting success. In his book *Uprising*, author Scott Goodson discusses the importance of building brands in the modern age. As Goodson stated in an interview in *Forbes* magazine: "Branding is fundamental. Branding is basic. Branding is essential. Building brands builds incredible value for companies and corporations."[419]

Just as good branding is necessary for the survival of a business, so it is necessary for the survival of a political party. The interconnectedness and obsession with image in the modern era has made marketing a crucial part of any campaign — whether in the private of public sector.

Re-branding is a tactic the Republican Party will need to employ if they want to capture the vote of the rising generation. According to The Center for Information and Research on Civic Learning and Engagement, around 21 percent of adult millennials cast a ballot during the 2014 midterm election — an alarmingly low statistic.[420] While the word "branding" may produce acid reflux in the stomachs of conservatives and Republicans alike, it is a necessary reality they must face if they want to survive. A successful branding of the Republican Party does not entail a rehashing of the glory days of former conservative leaders either — attaching #ReaganForever on every RNC Tweet has not done a lot to sway a younger vote.[421] Millennials don't truly understand the Republican sainting of Reagan because they were not alive then. While conservatives can appreciate what Reagan did for the image of the Republican Party in the past, the future of conservatism cannot subsist on borrowed light. To suggest that this older and previously once popular image of conservatism can be maintained and perpetuated by millennials is ridiculous. The current younger generation no longer faces the peril of a Soviet nuclear arms attack; they're concerned about other dilemmas such as determining the government's role in defining the word marriage.

Democrats have been successful in winning recent senate and presidential elections, not necessarily because they are more correct per say, but because they engage in conversations about current issues utilizing up-to-date technology and the megaphone of popular culture. Democrats don't necessarily have the best solutions for all of these modern day dilemma, — ranging from same-sex marriage to second amendment rights and isolationism versus involvement in the world — but they attract more support because of their willingness to think creatively about opening a dialogue to these situations. The left has mastered the sound bite, the trending internet meme, the kinetic-short-attention-span-over-simplification-of-complex-ideas-MTV approach to getting their ideas into the mainstream. Combine this ability with an ingenious ability to market and brand themselves while attracting hip young talent into their enterprise, and you've created an indomitable force to be reckoned with. As a consequence, Democrats control both the political dialogue and possess the tools necessary to maintain their power because they understand the branding and marketing processes.

Republicans mimic the branding tactics of Democrats when using Twitter, Facebook, YouTube, and other social media outlets to promote their causes, but the content Republican leadership produces is still not as flashy, attention-grabbing, or unique. Republicans have access to the necessary social media tools, but most of them do not use them properly for their intended audience. Without courage or creativity, it doesn't matter what tools an individual has access to.

The irony is that conservatives like Rush Limbaugh more or less created talk radio, which was the first serious assault on the left's media dominance. It was a creative tool used boldly to share conservatives' ideas. Some conservatives have also shown ingenuity in utilizing the blogosphere, Twitter, and new media (Breitbart, Drudge) to advance their message. What *is* missing are inroads to the entertainment world and the social media front, a critical component to messaging success.

A recent example of a failure in message marketing came from the hot-button debate on Obamacare. Former Senator Jim DeMint mounted a campaign to defund Obamacare, traveling state-to-state to speak to packed hotel ballrooms about the crusade. However, while DeMint's defund campaign gained traction amongst some, many Republicans saw the movement as more damaging when polls began to indicate that most Americans thought the GOP was to blame for the 2013 government shutdown. When DeMint commingled his anti-Obamacare rhetoric with the Republican-led government shutdown, he did not help matters. "We are not going to give in," he said. "One month, two months, three months — we are never going to give in. It's just that important.""[422] The Republican opposition to Obamacare is a natural reaction considering their belief in smaller government. However, conservative messages — perhaps even appealing ones — get lost in the angry uncompromising rhetoric of supposed conservative proponents such as DeMint's. Because the message is not marketed appealingly, and the true conservative feeling is lost in the rancor, the good that conservatism could do is choked off.

The party establishment does not take managing their image seriously enough. They assume that because conservative values speak for themselves, espousing a good work ethic and a patriotic fervor, nothing else needs to be said. They assume the mantra, "Republicans are good Americans" is already so appealing that there is no need to pour anymore energy into marketing their value system. However, this notion is false. Marketing a 1950s style of conservatism to a twenty-first century audience is bound to fail. This isn't to say that advocating the ideals of the past is the wrong approach, but the manner with which they do so falls flat or is even nonexistent. In order to solve this problem, the Republican Party should become more creative in how they engage the public. William F. Buckley Jr. knew how to do this. In a statement given by President Bush on the death of Mr. Buckley in 2008, he noted that "Bill Buckley was one of the founders of the modern conservative movement. He brought conservative thought into the political mainstream and helped lay the intellectual foundation for America's victory in the cold war…"[423] Buckley was able to articulate and make palpable conservative ideals in appealing ways to individuals in his era. Just as Buckley successfully revitalized the Republican Party in his era so Republicans need to do again.

The most effective messages are the ones that are creative, catchy, and relevant to their target audience. However, in some in some individuals' minds, especially for old-school conservatives, the realm of art is something that is reserved for the progressive. Progressives use art to communicate a political message through movies (especially), music, books and other media than conservatives seem to avoid. What Republicans fail to remember is just because an individual is conservative, it does not make them inept in the liberal arts. This false notion has been propagated by the media, though, in that they assume that political conservatism means that one is conservative on social issues as well. However, an individual can have a conservative approach in how he or she deals with the government's role, but at the same time, for example, be gay or pro-legalization of marijuana, identities that are typically associated with being progressive.

Some Republicans attribute the flocking of the masses (especially millennials) to becoming more ideologically progressive, as indicated by the overwhelming electoral success of President Obama in both the 2008 and 2012 election. In his 2009 book, *The Death of Conservatism*, Sam Tanenhaus discusses how conservatism is on the decline with the masses, losing popularity and traction with the electorate. Because the popularity of the conservatives has been dwindling — especially with youth[424] — Republicans did recognize years ago that they needed change in some capacity. Some assumed that this is a sign that conservatives needed to re-examine the bedrock of conservatism, thinking that perhaps conservatism was really out of date. However, this interpretation reveals only a surface-level understanding of the deeper problems. Rather than change the message of *what* conservatism is about, conservatives needed to change *how* they delivered their message. This is where the party began to err. Instead of understanding how art can be a platform to effectively communicate a message or truth to the masses, Republicans appear to believe that adopting such a tactic would morph them into progressives, or they believe the enterprise is too hard for them to break into. This results in many wasted opportunities for the party, opportunities that their political opponents continue to optimize at a greater level. The irony of the situation is that Republicans' obstinacy in using technology and the arts to disseminate their message to the masses forced the party into an unnecessary deviation from their original core values. Meaning they tried to change their content rather than the delivery of their message. This change, as evidenced in part by the birth of the Teas Party, has produced more dogmatic reactionaries and progressives rather than the desired effect of a revitalization of classic conservative principles. Before the party fractured, Republicans only required a more surface-level remodel, changing the "how" they functioned and becoming better at branding and marketing themselves. Instead, they fractured themselves internally, creating a problem that's more complicated and harder to solve. Republicans now need to get back to their conservative roots while simultaneously developing an effective marketing strategy on how to sell their principles more successfully.

Because of the current caustic tension existing between the Democrats and Republicans in Congress, neither side is willing to learn from the successes of the other. Instead of adopting and learning from Barack Obama's innovative use of the internet as seen in the 2008 presidential campaign, which gave him access to a more diverse and greater portion of the electorate, Republicans have become more defensive and contrary out of sheer stubbornness. There is something to be said for Obama's use of celebrities such as Alicia Keys and Oprah in order to sell Obamacare to the masses.[425] Republicans' hubris, rather than helping, ultimately damns the Republican cause instead of advancing it.

Republicans are drowning in denial. Outwardly they have become actively louder in their opposition to the Democrats, but most real passion has been channeled into movement politics instead of message innovation. This is often seen in rancorous rallies thrown by the Tea Party. For example, one might look to the many demonstrations outside of the Capitol to oppose the implementation of Obamacare. Additionally, Tea Party action groups initiate robocalls in which constituents are patched through to their Congressman with an automated call forwarding device. These are very efficient ways of communicating to a supposed conservative swell amongst the American people, but ultimately cannot be a lasting solution to fixing the deeper image issues facing The Republican Party. Tea Partiers can go into lengthy diatribes about why the Constitution and 1776 are important, but they struggle to correctly connect the dots between the past and the present and the situation of conservatism today, and they struggle to clearly communicate the importance of keeping conservative values alive today. Subsequently, the Republican Party's platform often devolves into ad-hominem attacks against Democrats as is seen in some of the raging fury directed against the Obama Administration.

After first stripping away the collective antagonism that has infiltrated the Republicans, the party must then begin to develop a sustainable marketing strategy. One of the main ways that Republicans can do this, as previously stated, is through becoming more involved in the arts community. However, to enact something unique amongst people risks facing ridicule and intrusive questioning upon suspicion of conservatism's integrity. Republicans are frequently seen (and rightfully to an extent) as undermining the survival and prominence of the arts. In fact, in 2011, a group of Republicans calling themselves the Republican Study Group revealed a plan to cut federal funding for the arts down zero.[426] Even though the journey towards reconciling the art world with the tenets of conservatism proves to be very rocky, it is necessary. And while considerable tension exists at times between conservatives and artistic sentiments, this does not indicate that tension should be eliminated, but that tension should be struggled with and must endure, even as a paradox that remains resolute at times. Regardless of however Republican leadership goes about changing the people's perception of the party, they still need to communicate a more unified agenda and fix their image.

Republican Senator and Tea Party member Mike Lee (Utah), argues that the Republican Party "may not seem to have much of a relevant reform message at all. That is the real reason the GOP is in such internal disarray today."[427] Some new conservative reform agenda is needed, according to Lee. However, it is Lee's own extreme right side of the party that has forced Republicans into a nay-saying band of obstructionists and critics who claimed that their primary mission during President Obama's second term in office is to simply say "No." Moderates, negotiators, compromisers, and would-be politicians have been silenced and immobilized by the pressures from the party's far right and its factions influence on their electoral bases. This particular political group may or may not offer positive contribution to American government, but the consequences of their negative influence upon a good portion of the voting public are career-ending and government-breaking. Sounding like a progressive conservative rather than a Tea Partier, Lee says that "first, we need a new, comprehensive anti-poverty and upward-mobility agenda designed not simply to help people in poverty, but to help and empower them to get out."[428]

With progressives and movement politics throughout both parties, it is difficult to distinguish many Republicans from Democrats. This confusion reveals itself in the ease with which members of either party have crossed over to the other. However, when Tea Partiers such as Senator Lee cannot readily be distinguished from progressives within their own Republican Party— and even sound as much— or more like a Democrat than any traditional Republican, let alone an authentic conservative, the situation becomes more confusing and fluid.

Despite this fractiousness of the Republican Party, Republicans still had electoral victories by "conservatives" of varying stripes, but a fractured party couldn't last. Ultimately, these same internal factions began to drive the party into an all-out identity crises by spring 2014. Hearkening back to the early years of America's modern conservative movement, the 1950s Communist turned Republican, Whittaker Chambers, was now quoted: "If the Republican Party cannot get some grip of the actual world we live in, and from it generalize and actively promote a program that means something to masses of people —why, somebody else will. There will be nothing to argue . . . The Republican Party will become like one of those dark little shops which apparently never sell anything."[429] Obviously, Chambers had not left ideological thinking behind when he abandoned communism. Instead, he urged the then fledgling conservative movement to transform the GOP into an ideological party complete with programmatic activism and the kind of salesmanship that appeals to mass movements of popular support. Now, some sixty years later, Republicans have begun to diagnose a similar situation for themselves. Movement conservatism throughout the intervening years has brought the party back to square one in terms of its lack of a clear, singular identity. Its fragmented membership is unable to rally unity to support the ideas and policies that are required for shaping any such identity. Republican candidates have been campaigning with superficial slogans for some time instead of making real appeals of substance to the American people and their interests. After President Obama's election to a second term in office, Republicans found themselves "engaged in a fresh bout of soul searching" that seems to have accomplished little in preparation for the 2016 presidential election. Divisions now exist within the party that are deemed serious enough to "bring it down. The Tea Party faction has crystalized widespread disenchantment with the mainstream Republican Party."[430]

The fractiousness of the Republican Party becomes especially apparent when assessing the wide ideological span of the 2016 Republican candidates. How can the likes of Donald Trump, Ted Cruz, Carly Fiorina, Marco Rubio, Jeb Bush, and Ben Carson all exist under the same party umbrella?

The candidate mixture created a media frenzy phenomenon. Some decried the estranged mixture of candidates, while others celebrated the frenzied circus and ruckus that the party has found itself in. Executive Editor of *The Daily Caller*, Tucker Carlson, shared his frustration and summed up many citizenry's feelings on the GOP's identity crisis in his widely shared article titled *Donald Trump Is Shocking, Vulgar and Right*.

"It turns out the GOP wasn't simply out of touch with its voters; the party had no idea who its voters were or what they believed. For decades, party leaders and intellectuals imagined that most Republicans were broadly libertarian on economics and basically neoconservative on foreign policy."[431]

In fact, the neo-conservative element of the Party appears to be enjoying a renaissance as we approach the end of Barack Obama's presidency; the neocons are up and running again. And Former Vice President Dick Cheney is regaining influence among many throughout the party, rebounding from what appeared to be a disastrous end of his political career. More than anything, however, it is supposed to be President Obama's actions, or lack of them, in the recent past against ISIS and the collapse of any American victory in Iraq that has rekindled neo-conservatives to life, propelling them back into influence within the Republican Party. Thanks to Obama, "it's suddenly springtime for neocons" once more.[432] Still, the GOP's vision of the future in the Middle East goes far beyond the defeat of ISIS in Iraq and ultimate success in Afghanistan; it goes far beyond any policies or planning that President Obama might contemplate. Neo-cons continue to dream of regime change throughout the world and of the domino effect they still hope to create for "democracy" in the Middle East. Iraq and Afghanistan remain merely the first to topple for such a movement to take place, just as they have been since the first Gulf War, according to the neo-conservative mind.

Conclusion

Elephants in the Forest

During the past half century, we have seen authentic American conservatism increasingly eclipsed by the political rhetoric of big plans and grand schemes. We have heard its voice grow dim while the voices of movement politics have dominated our political landscape, both on the left and on the right. American politics has become all movement and generally progressive. With this imbalance, we have overshadowed authentic conservatism and prevented it from playing its role of moderation and stability. Subsequently, social demands and desires have become preeminent in public life, eliminating the political practices of negotiation and compromise so that the political pursuit of the good and its elevation of human being has been degraded into the cultural and economic pursuit of happiness as the satisfaction of base desires. The loss of authentic conservatism in America has brought upon us the degradation of politics.

Conservatives adopted progressive tactics in politics, advocating political and social movement as much as their liberal adversaries, developing a "progressive conservatism" as early as the Eisenhower administration. This departure from authentic conservatism resulted from the development of an ideological conservatism in the 1950s, thought necessary by Republicans in order for them to compete politically with progressive Democrats and to regain relevance for themselves in American politics. This runs counter to true conservatism and its origins as an anti-ideological response to the rise of modern liberalism and the unintended consequences that are risked by blueprints and grand plans for rapid change that characterize all ideologies. The ultimate political outcome of this conflict between conservatism and "progressive conservatism" is that Americans are left without any real alternatives to ideological movement politics, and authentic American conservatives are left without any real voice. Instead, they are lost in the fray of the Republican Party's internal factions.

A problematic dynamic of conflict has arisen between properly social and traditional political concerns due to the social focus of progressive politics. What passes for politics now is the satisfaction of private desires and the affairs of society rather than the accomplishment of public goods, which are the matters of true politics. Society and economics dominate the "political" arena, degrading it into struggles for "mere life," meaning the securing of food, clothing, and shelter. These are base primary goods of animal life rather than the higher goods of politics and the "good life" that raises us above the animals and characterizes authentic human being. Progressive politics only respond to the economic and social desires of "mere life," thus American politics are degraded. Balance is required between authentic conservatism and the movement politics of progressivism in order to keep politics lively and human beings attaining political as well as social goods.

Ronald Reagan rejected conservative views of history and progress and instead implemented policies of sudden and dramatic change. He imposed economic blueprints regardless of unintended consequences, and his foreign policy pushed hard to end the Cold War quickly. The first generation of neo-conservatives rose to national prominence and influence within the context of this foreign policy. Ultimately, the social concerns of security and the economy prevailed over political virtues such as justice and moderation during the Reagan presidency. Thus, the growing dominance of the social over the political was further aggravated, the degradation of the political deepened, and progressivism became dominant within the

Republican Party as the avenue to supposed success and prosperity for America. Here we see the end of truly conservative alternatives to progressivism in America, even as we see the end of viable political alternatives to the cultural and social dominance of American liberal democracy.

With Bill Clinton's election to the White House, the Republican Party's movement conservatives turned exclusively to Congress for power. Here we see movement conservatism and particularly "progressive conservatism" beginning to flex its muscles with open and unabashed departures from authentic conservatism, which it began to renounce and denounce as outdated and outmoded. Newt Gingrich emerged during the Reagan presidency with a "hard movement conservative line," eventually to set himself up as the leader of Republicans as they took control of Congress in the 90s for the first time since the 1950s. They did so through Gingrich's extremely ideological "progressive conservatism." Gingrich worked to eliminate moderates from the Republican Party as creatures of the past. After his rise and fall, Tom Delay took over leadership of the Republican Congress and continued its movement against Clinton's presidency. Delay's less ideological, less principled "progressive conservatism," focused more upon power than ideals when compared with Gingrich's leadership. This power-oriented unprincipled progressivism led to corruption and the further degradation of American politics. It also led to the end of Delay's political career.

As president, George W. Bush was an idealistic movement oriented conservative who found himself caught in a perfect storm. His natural orientation toward movement politics aligned with his Christian millennialism and a religious language of good and evil to shape his political rhetoric. However, his inexperience with and ignorance of foreign policy left him at the mercy of a new generation of neo-conservatives who spoke the same language of good and evil but with different meaning and purpose. They were able to take advantage of Bush's dependence upon them while dovetailing their own rhetoric with the President's religious language in order to manipulate both the President and his Christian Right base. As well, Dick Cheney manipulated his way into the vice presidency on his own terms, establishing himself practically as co-president with Bush. His participation in meetings, agenda setting, and policy formulation as vice president was unprecedented. Cheney placed neo-conservative colleagues who had served with him in former administrations into key cabinet and policy positions.

Thus, the events of September 11, 2001, found a Bush administration ready to respond with a variety of "conservative" motivations. The wars in Afghanistan and Iraq became expressions of the neo-conservatives' democratic movement conservatism and President Bush's Christian progressive conservatism. The wars were supported almost unanimously and uncritically by progressive Democrats. Here we see the ultimate fallout of the imbalance created by almost completely progressive and movement oriented politics. There were no authentically conservative voices or influences that could stop imprudent ideological political action or prevent the myriad of unintended consequences that continue to plague American society and politics to this day. Slowly, President Bush gained his independence from those who manipulated him and his policies. One by one the administration's significant neo-conservatives were forced to resign or were relocated away from the President until finally only Cheney was left within Bush's sphere of influence. Eventually, President Bush even cut Cheney off, refusing to take calls from the vice president, to meet with him, or to otherwise talk with him at all during the latter part of his presidency.[433]

Emerging around the time of the end of the Bush regime, the Tea Party further complicated the Republican Party's inner factionalism. This division has created an identity crisis for the Republican Party during the past few years. With the still increasing fractiousness within the GOP, the Tea Party has become more of a hindrance than a help to the Republican Party. Tea Partiers are radical reactionaries, looking to restore the conditions of an imagined "golden age" in America, a restoration that would dramatically change the American political and social landscapes in a revolutionary manner. There is nothing conservative about this. The overlap of Tea Party membership with Christian Right supporters has energized a portion of the American population that had lost its voice with the demise of the Moral Majority and the subsequent rise and fall of the Christian Coalition within the Republican Party. Establishment Republicans who have become progressive conservatives were scared off by the high watermark of the Christian Right within the Party and they began to marginalize them, particularly in the public image of the party. These important and captive Republicans have now regained influence and control of much of the party's agenda through their development of the Tea Party and its public rhetoric. However, new re-branding ideas are necessary in order to revitalize and give voice to authentic conservatives. Only this may reinvigorate popular faith in the Republican Party—especially with millennial voters.

This is how things stand well into the 2016 election process. We have moved from the progressive conservatives and neo-cons of the Bush era, who were trying to establish an identity for the Republican Party and for America, to the current multiplicity of identities in the party that crash into each other as they scramble for direction and a new identity.[434] A new "reform conservatism" seemed to hold some promise of return, at least in the direction of authentic conservatism, but its proponents have left their ideas ill-defined and also seem oblivious to the fact that the party has been movement-oriented and largely progressive for decades now. It seems all too likely that we will see only another version of progressive conservatism emerging from this "new" movement.[435] We wonder if the Tea Party/Christian Right might hold together long enough to break away from the establishment Republicans who have controlled the agenda of the conservative movement in a progressive mode for too long and too firmly for the reactionary elements of the party to remain with them much longer. All of this points to the continued domination of the social over the political and toward continued and increasing imbalance in American politics as it threatens to continue on as perpetually progressive- and movement-oriented.

Since the Bush presidency, Republicans have mostly nominated progressive conservative candidates who appealed to the moderates of the party, candidates who did not carry great support from the Christian Right or libertarian factions of the party. These factions have supported their own challengers for Republican nominations. The Christian Right has been especially significant in withholding its full support from Republican presidential candidates John McCain and Mitt Romney. Their preferred challengers, Mike Huckabee and Rick Santorum respectively, were equally unable to win the support of the important moderate and progressive establishment factions of the GOP. Having failed twice to defeat Democrat Barrack Obama in campaigns for the presidency, the Republican Party is now more divided and complex than ever before.

Recently, while putting out feelers for his possible run for the presidency, Governor John Kasich of Ohio was told that his fellow Republican, Governor Scott Walker of Wisconsin, was more conservative than himself. Kasich took umbrage at this and roared, "I think I have the right to define what conservatism is." An eleven-minute tirade followed as Kasich lectured on a variety of economic, moral, and cultural issues as seen through his "conservative" eyes.[436] Newt Gingrich continues to support his once ideal Republican Congressman: "John Kasich is in some ways the most intuitively innovative person in the Republican Party since Jack Kemp . . . He is very conservative, but he is very unorthodox."[437] Once known in Washington as a fiscal hawk, Kasich now stresses his Christian faith and criticizes Republicans for "waging war on the poor." Sheryl Stolberg of *The New York Times* reported that religion pulls Kasich "to the left on poverty issues while he tacks reliably right on most others." Symbolic of his party's identity crisis, "you don't know which John Kasich is going to show up."[438] Ohio Democratic strategist Jerry Austin said "[Kasich is] almost like a multiple in terms of personalities."[439] His presidential bid may have been helped by his political grasp of Ohio, but he lacked conservative bona fides despite Gingrich's appraisal. He is Gingrich's type of conservative, which is no conservative at all.

The Tea Party showed strength in Congressional and State elections, but a Tea Party candidate didn't capture the Republican nomination for President in the 2016 campaign—Donald Trump did. However, the Tea Party paved the way for a candidate like Donald Trump to become the Republican nominee. It remains equally doubtful that another moderate establishment nominee will enjoy strong support from the Tea Party or other far right elements of the party. The Republicans need future candidates who can cut across these factional lines and unify enough of the party across the board to provide Republicans with a new and clear identity. This is a difficult bill to fill, however, as their identity crises is rooted in differences that are neither superficial nor transient. It's a deeply rooted and fairly permanent problem for the Republican Party. As former policy adviser and chief of speechwriting for President George W. Bush, Michael Gerson and Peter Wehner, a senior fellow at the Ethics and Public Policy Center noted: "This is not just bad news for the Republican Party; it is bad news for the country. As much as any time in recent history, America needs a strong, vibrant party…" [440] American needs an authentically conservative alternative to movement and progressive politics of the Left as well as the Right. We need this in order to create real choice as well as balance and moderation for the restoration of politics proper in American public life.[441] Now more than ever, negotiation and compromise, real politics, are needed as we face Congressional gridlock and an increasingly divided political culture.

Many Americans have been disappointed with President Obama's refusal or inability to keep his 2008 campaign promises. These include many of his supporters in and out of the Democrat Party. There has been disappointment, as well, with President Obama for not living up to the Nobel Peace Prize awarded him at the beginning of his first term, an award given him not for what he had accomplished, but for the expectations and hopes of what he might accomplish but has since failed to meet. Still, he won reelection in 2012 despite these disappointments, and the disgruntled rumblings amongst his original supporters. As opposed to being seen as a radical transformer of politics or the ultra progressive that his opponents have painted him to be, President Obama won over mainstream America during his first term: "The majority that voted for him [in 2012] were put off by the radical changes advocated by the Republican market and religious fundamentalists."[442] While establishment Republicans and anti-establishment populists in the GOP, such as members of the Tea Party, are said to have long hated each other, in the past they have known how to win and rule together by endlessly postponing the policy measures that they really cared about. The Republican coalition was held together by internal negotiation and compromise, even as its members refused to engage in such political behavior with their Democratic counterparts.

As Michael Smerconish of CNN has reminded us, political parties exist to win elections, not to express ideological principles.[443] Of course, these very party dynamics have excluded authentic conservatives from political relevance because power has overwhelmed principles and movement politics have eclipsed conservatism. An increasing number of American voters have become "independents" in an exodus from the GOP toward the center, thus moving establishment Republicans toward the center in efforts to recapture these votes. At the opposite end of the Republican Party spectrum, ideological extremists such as Tea Partiers and libertarians have shown that they can win Primaries but generally cannot win elections. Thus, the Republican Party establishment has resisted them for fear of losing Congressional seats and political power at all levels of government. This means that the party has become progressive and has rejected reactionary policies for the most part. The GOP's public face has been progressive conservative. Oftentimes these politicians have pursued liberal policies (the right things for liberal Democrats), but for fiscally conservative motives (the wrong reasons according to the same liberals). California has decriminalized marijuana because it has become too expensive for its government to prosecute offenders. Colorado is currently celebrating the tax revenue raised by its legal marijuana sales as first reports come in, perhaps revealing something of a similar motivation as California beneath its drug law changes. In Missouri, judges are provided with the costs of incarceration prior to sentencing criminals and are turning to alternative punishments in order to save money for the state—a new sort of consideration in their judgments and sentencing. Principles are being abandoned for economic reasons rather than for the sake of compromise or politics and justice. The preeminence of social needs and concerns over politics is deepening. Again, securing "mere life" prevails over the pursuit of the "good life" and its virtues.

Elephants on the Rampage

According to David Brooks, movement conservatives are losing support in foreign policy, their original mainstay. "Today it's harder to have faith in rapid progress," he reports. However, this does not point to a return of politics; "It is less about reforms that will improve all lives and more about unadorned struggles for power." We see no resurgence of true conservatism here in the rejection of rapid progress. Rather than careful contemplation of alternatives and negotiation guided by public virtue, we see instead that "tough guys do well. Cooperative skills are less valued while confrontational skills are more valued." Dictatorial leadership thrives now that "electorates get a little uglier when faith in progress declines."[444] Public virtue continues to wane as security becomes the preeminent value of American political culture. This, despite Benjamin Franklin's warning long ago that, paraphrased, asserts that a people who will trade liberty (once America's governing ideal) for security is worthy of neither.

The President of Utah Valley University, Matthew S. Holland, published a book in 2007 about civic charity as the essence of America's true public virtue. This civic virtue originates within Western Civilization's Judeo-Christian Biblical tradition, but transcends this tradition in the American experience.[445] Quite brilliantly, Holland shows that civic charity, an attitude of tolerance and fraternity, runs throughout the American political tradition as "bonds of affection" by which we are tied together as a people. Holland reveals a kinder, gentler side of Jonathan Winthrop, the supposed extremely rigid and domineering Puritan Governor of Massachusetts Colony.[446] Despite his reputation for ruling with an iron fist, Winthrop displayed charity in his political actions regarding religious and political dissenters such as Roger Williams. Rather than extreme punishment or execution of these different-minded, free thinkers, Winthrop let them leave the colony and move to form another equally original American home.[447]

Holland shows that this charitable streak existed in Winthrop from before the Puritan beginning in America. Winthrop's famous speech aboard the Puritan flagship Arabella, "A Model of Christian Charity," gave us our famous image of ourselves as "a city upon a hill." Public charity is promoted throughout this speech as the key to successful political life in America before the Puritans set foot upon the soil of the New World.[448]

Lest we attach this sentiment to Puritans or even Christians only, Holland then shows that Thomas Jefferson displayed this same civic charity as central to his own public virtue.[449] Denounced as an infidel while campaigning for the American presidency, Jefferson's sentiments transcend their Biblical origins and their early American Puritan expression. Jefferson is famous for his secularization of Christian morality. He rewrote the New Testament in such a way as to remove all miracles and mysteries in order to provide a more universal rendition of Judeo-Christian virtue. The Jefferson Bible gives us an authentic and original American secular morality and public virtue of civic charity.[450] Canadian political philosopher George Grant asserts that "it is the case that in the western world what remnants of sacred restraints still linger in the minds of men are most often connected with the practice of the two religions, Judaism and Christianity, which alone are indigenous to the western world."[451]

Jefferson's actions as President of the United States are reminiscent of Winthrop's civic charity, but free of the Puritan contradictions of rigidity and extremism from which this public virtue emerged. Jefferson hones civic charity as a public virtue for all Americans, through his own extremism in an opposite direction from the Puritans.[452] Holland chooses his iconic models carefully and wisely, showing us that civic charity exists in the most extreme of America's religious heritage and equally so in the supposed most extremely secular of our Iconic Founding figures. He moves finally to Abraham Lincoln to show the greatest expressions of our authentic public virtue of civic charity.[453]

Caught in the most extreme tensions and violence in our history, Lincoln emerges with a clearly Biblical but equally universal voice of American civic charity as our public virtue. Unattached to any particular religion and entirely devoted to American union, Lincoln displays the most sympathetic expressions of American fraternity through his majestic political speech during the Civil War. Civic charity emerges clearly from Lincoln's Second Inaugural Address as the guiding sentiment for peace in America's political future.[454] This Address is a close second to the Gettysburg Address as the single greatest political speech in American history, perhaps even in world history.

In the thick of civil warfare, the Gettysburg Address re-baptizes the nation in her "bonds of affection" from which she was born. We are born again in this short and perfect speech. Patterned after the much longer ancient funeral oration of Pericles during the Peloponnesian Wars, and delivered in the style of an American jeremiad, Lincoln renews our Founding sentiments and points us toward our future.[455] He does so with speech thoroughly immersed in civic charity, renewing America's political tradition and her public virtue. His Second Inaugural Address gives explicit expression to these sentiments of civic charity in unmistakable language. Our first Republican President gives voice to our national essence, an authentic conservative voice of preservation and renewal of the American political tradition and the public virtue by which we live together and politic together in a truly political community. Lincoln's preservation of the Union is a conservative salvation of American politics and a renewal of the American spirit, forward-thinking but rooted in the past. His is one of the greatest examples of truly conservative change, demonstrating the ability of American conservatism to adapt and progress without detaching ourselves from our moorings and setting ourselves adrift on the currents of rootless progressivism or reactionary revolution.[456]

Moving to twentieth-century politics, Hannah Arendt has shown us the way forward out of the mistakes of political movements and ideologies. Jonathan Schell's brief commentary upon Arendt's work stresses a politics of forgiveness that emerges from her work.[457] This involves a spirit within the hearts of citizens, rather than a formula for political policy or a doctrine of political power. According to Arendt, it is "with word and deed [that] we insert ourselves into the human world and this insertion is like a second birth."[458] Schell explains that the "foundation of a political order that guarantees the continuity of life would be a true 'second birth'—a rebirth."[459] The reminiscence of Lincoln here is profound.

What has been done is done; political actions stand as accomplished facts. "But there is a remedy" to having to live with the mistakes, Schell tells us. "It is forgiveness." Having been subjected to the unintended consequences of political movements, "forgiveness overcomes the irreversibility of action and breaks the endless chain of its consequences, releasing the sons from the sins of the fathers."[460] It is through political forgiveness that we are able to live with political action yet not be bound by the outcomes of politics and policies forever. The willingness to forgive frees us to act yet retain our freedom from perpetual consequences of action. Forgiveness frees us to be political, in other words. "Forgiveness, in short, plays the same role within actions that action plays in life and nature: it is the source of freedom."[461] We see how intimately political forgiveness resides in Lincoln's "new birth of freedom" and in the civic charity that delivers it.

This rebirth was not accomplished by bullets and bayonets that so painfully accompanied it, but by the political sentiments of civic charity in our public virtue that transcends the blood and pain and sacrifice of this nativity. The spirit of political forgiveness, the willingness to own our actions including our mistakes and to move beyond them, is a close companion to civic charity. Both of these attitudes or sentiments reside within the souls of true conservatives. Responsibility, reparation, and recognition, accepting what we have done and carefully repairing our mistakes in a spirit of mutual recognition of citizenship and our belonging together, these are the motive forces of authentic conservatism in America. Bringing these attitudes to bear upon political action before it is taken moderates that action. Applying these sentiments after political action keeps politics alive and allows us to move forward with freedom and continuity as a people.

The courage of moderation is, then, the third virtue in a triad of virtues that form American public virtue: civic charity, political forgiveness, and the courage of moderation to shape America's public virtue. A professor at Indiana University, Aurelia Craiutu, in 2012 gave eloquent voice to this courage of moderation as a "virtue for courageous minds."[462] Matching a commitment to liberty with a concern for moderation is the conservative way of politics. This combination is accomplished through the lessons of experience and practice rather than abstract speculation. American experience, our tradition, informs authentic conservatism rather than our being guided by ideological blueprints for action or the rhetoric of movement politics. At least this should be the case for conservatives proper in America.

Authentic conservatism practiced with civil charity means that "in politics one can make sensible decisions even in the darkest of times and most political questions admit of a middle, which can be found through trial and error."[463] This is conservative politics, the careful seeking of the moderate way forward. It is moved by the courage of moderation, the courage to resist the fantastic promises of the progressive fast-forward into the future or the sentimental security of the reactionary back to the future promises of the radical right. "This union of life with measure, of spirit with reasonableness, makes a moderate (and middling) mind at once firm and flexible, full of common sense, vivacity, and buoyancy."[464] Hearkening back to Edmund Burke's birth of modern conservatism, authentic conservatives "maintain a healthy dose of skepticism toward any form of zealotry and reject all attempts to impose the absolute rule of a single idea or political principle."[465] Moral conservatives may have preferred policies and desires for change, as do Constitutional conservatives, but political conservatives have a preferred attitude toward political change that ensures productive, stable government. Finally, whether in government or in opposition, authentic conservatives act with moderation and govern themselves according to virtue. They lead by example as well as by precept. Conservatives have the courage of moderation, which is political wisdom that leads toward justice, meaning the political good. These four cardinal virtues are practiced by conservatives in America under the umbrella of her public virtue of civic charity. A renewal of this virtue in America and of American conservatism would help restore politics in America and the pursuit of the good to her people.

About the Authors

SARA JARMAN is currently a law student at Brigham Young University's J. Reuben Clark Law School. She was previously a journalist and online content manager for KSL.com, a NBC affiliate and top-rated local news network and website. She also covered news during Election 2014, publishing pieces on topics ranging from various candidates to issues on the ballot. She has also published articles in *The Daily Caller, The Hill*, and in various other publications. She is an Honors graduate from Brigham Young University, having written her Honors Thesis on the subject of this book.

BRENT GILCHRIST held a doctorate in Political Science and Political Philosophy from Carleton University. He taught for 16 years at Brigham Young University, Pittsburg State University and Carleton University. He was the author of *Cultus Americanus: Varieties of the Liberal Tradition in American Political Culture 1620-1865* (Lexington Press, 2006; rpt. 2007). Gilchrist taught political philosophy in the Political Science Department at Utah State University in Logan, Utah, as well as teaching online courses for Utah State. Brent Gilchrist passed away in September of 2016.

Citation Index

1. Aristotle, *The Politics*. Edited and revised by Trevor J. Saunders. Translated by T. A. Sinclair (Harmondsworth: Penguin, 1981); E. J. Dionne Jr., *Why Americans Hate Politics* (New York: Simon & Schuster, 2004).
2. Hannah Arendt, *The Human Condition* (Chicago: Univ. of Chicago Press, 1958), throughout: see p. 33 for example; Hannah Arendt, *The Promise of the Politics* (Random House 2005), throughout: see p.108 for example.
3. Arendt, *The Human Condition*, p.33.
4. *Ibid.*, p.40.
5. *Ibid.*, p.38.
6. Aristotle, *Politics,* Book One.
7. Arendt, *The Human Condition*, p.40; Arendt, *The Promise of the Politics*, p.17.
8. Michael Oakeshott, "On Being Conservative," in Michael Oakeshott, *Rationalism in Politics and Other Essays* (Indianapolis: Liberty Press, 1991).
9. *Ibid.*
10. *Ibid.*
11. Michael Oakeshott, "Rationalism in Politics," in Michael Oakeshott, *Rationalism in Politics and Other Essays* (Indianapolis: Liberty Press, 1991).
12. Leon P. Baradat, *Political Ideologies: Their Origins and Impact* 6th ed. (Upper Saddle River: Prentice Hall, 1997); Isaac Kramnick and Frederick M. Watkins, *The Age of Ideology Political Thought, 1750 to the Present.* 2nd ed. (Englewood Cliffs: Prentice-Hall, 1976).

13. Edmund Burke, *Reflections on the Revolution in France* (BiblioLife, 2008), p.
14. Willard A. Mullins, "On the Concept of Ideology in Political Science," American Political Science Review 66 (1972), pp.498-510.
15. Brent Gilchrist, *Cultus Americanus: Varieties of the Liberal Tradition in America 1600-1865* (Lanham, MD: Lexington Books, 2006), p.70, 116.
16. Harry V. Jaffa, *A New Birth of Freedom: Abraham Lincoln and the Coming of the Civil War* (Lanham, MD: Rowman & Littlefield, 2000); Gary Wills, Lincoln at Gettysburg: The Words That Remade America (New York: Simon & Schuster, 2000).
17. Frederick Jackson Turner, *The Frontier in American History* (New York: Henry Holt Co., 1958); Horace Greeley, *New York Tribune*, 13 July 1865 (rephrasing first use of the phrase by John Basbone Lane Soule, *Terre Haute Express*, 1851).
18. Kenneth M. Dolbeare and Michael S. Cummings, "Populism," in Dobeare and Cummings eds., *American Political Thought* 6th ed. (Washington D. C.: CQ Press, 2010), pp.334 339.
19. Martin J. Sklar, "Periodization and Historiography: Studying American Political Development in the Progressive Era, 1890s-1916" in *Studies in American Political Development* 5 (Fall 1991), 173-213; Heather Cox Richardson, *To Make Men Free: A History of the Republican Party* (New York: Basic Books, 2014), pp.139-142; Robert Allen Rutland, *The Republicans: From Lincoln to Bush* (Columbia, MO: Univ. of Missouri Press, 1996), p.144.
20. John D. Buenker, John C. Burnham, and Robert M. Crunden, *Progressivism* (Schenkman Books, 1977); Kenneth M. Dolbeare and Michael S. Cummings, "Progressivism," in Dolbeare and Cummings eds., *American Political Thought* 6th ed. (Washington D. C.: CQ Press, 2010), pp.425-431; "Frederick W. Taylor," in *Ibid.*, pp.431-438; "Woodrow Wilson," in *Ibid.*, pp.438-443.
21. Richardson, *To Make Men Free*, pp.201-203.
22. Rutland, *The Republicans*, pp.208-209, 214-215; Richardson, *To Make Men Free*, pp.224, 231-238.

23. Henry Grady Weaver, *The Mainspring of Human Progress* (New York: Henry Holt & Co., 1958).
24. Zbigniew Brzezinski and Samuel P. Huntington, *Political Power: U.S.A./U.S.S.R.* (New York: Viking, 1965), pp.17, 23-24, 56.
25. Dolbeare and Cummings, "Franklin D. Roosevelt," in Dolbeare and Cummings eds., *American Political Thought* 6th ed., pp.452-466.
26. Arthur Larson, *Eisenhower: The President Nobody Knows* (New York: Scribner, 1968).
27. Robert Welch, *The Politician* (Belmont, Mass: Robert Welch, 1963); Robert Welch, *The Blue Book of the John Birch Society* (Belmont, MASS: Western Island, 1959).
28. *Why We Fight*. Sony Pictures, Eugene Jarecki Writer and Director (January 2005).
29. Barry Goldwater, *The Conscience of a Conservative* (New York: Victor Publishing, 1960).
30. Richardson, *To Make Men Free*, pp.291-292; Garry Wills, *Reagan's America* (New York: Viking Penguin, 1987), pp.445-447, 466-477; Thomas Frank, *What's the Matter With Kansas: How Conservatives Won the Heart of America* (New York: Metropolitan Books, 2004), pp.6-7.
31. Ed Gillespie and Bob Schellhas, eds. *Contract With America: The Bold Plan by Rep. Newt Gingrich, Rep. Dick Armey and the House Republicans to Change the Nation* (New York: Random House, 1994).
32. Michael Patrick Leahy, *Covenant of Liberty: The Ideological Origins of the Tea Party Movement* (New York: Broadside Books, 2012).
33. Corey Robin, *The Reactionary Mind: Conservatism From Burke to Sarah Palin* (New York: Oxford Univ. Press, 2011), pp.55, 248; Jill Lepore, *The Whites of Their Eyes: The Tea Party's Revolution and the Battle Over American History* (Princeton: Princeton Univ. Press, 2010).
34. Noel O'Sullivan, *Conservatism* (London: J. M. Dent & Sons, 1976; rpt. 1983); John Kekes, *Case for Conservatism* (Ithaca: Cornell Univ. Press, 1998).
35. Richardson, *To Make Men Free*, pp.1-24; Rutland, *The Republicans*. pp.1-15.

36. Harry Jaffa, *A New Birth of Freedom*; Wills, *Lincoln at Gettysburg*; Matthew S. Holland, *Bonds of Affection: Civic Charity and the Making of America; Winthrop, Jefferson, and Lincoln* (Georgetown University Press, 2007).
37. Russell Kirk, *The Conservative Mind*, 2nd ed. Rev. (Chicago: Regnery, 1953), p.5.
38. Burke, *Reflections on the Revolution in France*, pp.5-8.
39. *Ibid.*, pp.5-8.
40. Brzezinzki and Huntington, *Political Power*, pp.17, 23-24, 56.
41. Samuel Huntington, "Conservatism as an Ideology," *American Political Science Review* 51 (1957).
42. Russell Kirk, *The American Cause* (Wilmington, DA: ISI Books, 2002; rpt.2012), pp.2-3, 121-122.
43. Huntington, "Conservatism as an Ideology."
44. Curtis White, *The Science Delusion: Asking the Big Questions in a Culture of Easy Answers* (Brooklyn: Melville House, 2013).
45. American Psychological Association. "Coburn Amendment Restricts NSF Political Science Funding," *Psychological Science Agenda* (April 2013).
46. Richardson, *To Make Men Free,* pp.139-142; Rutland, *The Republicans,* p.144; Buenker and Crunden, *Progressivism*; Dolbeare and Cummings, "Progressivism," pp.425-431; Dolbeare and Cummings, "Frederick W. Taylor," pp.431-438; Dolbeare and Cummings, "Woodrow Wilson," pp.438-443; Dolbeare and Cummings, "Franklin D. Roosevelt," pp.452-466.
47. Larson, Arthur. *A Republican Looks at His Party* (New York: Harper & Bros., 1956).
48. William Martin, *With God on Our Side: The Rise of the Religious Right in America* (New York: Broadway Books, 1996), pp.80-83; Richardson, *To Make Men Free,* pp.268-270; Sam Tanenhaus, *The Death of Conservatism: A Movement and Its Consequences* (New York: Random House, 2010), pp.43-48, 58-63; Barry Goldwater, *The Conscience of a Conservative* (New York: Victor Publishing, 1960).

49. A look at the 1996 GOP Party Convention reveals how overbearing were the Religious Right on stage and television. The radical impression made by the Convention scared the mainstream of the Party and the near public invisibility of the extreme right at future GOP conventions speaks to the reaction of the most powerful forces within the party.
50. Kirk, *The American Cause*, p.11.
51. Richard White and Patricia Nelson Limerick, *The Frontier in American Culture* (Oakland: Univ. of California Press, 1994).
52. Tocqueville, Democracy in America; Paul A. Rahe, *Soft Despotism, Democracy's Drift: Montesquieu, Rousseau, Tocqueville, and the Modern Prospect* (New Haven: Yale Univ. Press, 2009).
53. William F. Buckley Jr., *God and Man at Yale* (Chicago: Henry Regnery Co., 1951); William F. Buckley Jr. ed. *National Review* (increasingly influential magazine founded by Buckley to counter the homogenous liberal voice of American public life, included important contributors of diverse "conservative" stripes).
54. James Madison, *Federalist Papers* Nos. 10, 51.
55. Richardson, *To Make Men Free*, pp.239-244.
56. As quoted in Tanenhaus, *The Death of Conservatism*, p.39.
57. Rutland, *The Republicans*, p.215.
58. President Dwight Eisenhower, "Atoms for Peace Speech" (December 8, 1953), United Nations General Assembly.
59. Larson, *A Republican Looks at His Party*; Dean A. Acheson, *Democrat Looks at His Party* (New York: Harper & Bros.: 1955).
60. *Ibid.*
61. Goldwater, *The Conscience of a Conservative*.
62. John S. Saloma III, Ominous Politics: The New Conservative Labyrinth (New York: Hill and Wang, 1984), pp.39-40; Richardson, *To Make Men Free*, pp.246-249; Tanenhaus, *The Death of Conservatism*, pp.52-53.
63. *Ibid.*, pp.52-55.
64. Buckley, *God and Man at Yale*.
65. Carl Bogus, "Who's Killing Conservatism." *The American Prospect* (September 19 2009).

66. William F. Buckley Jr., *Keeping the Tablets: Modern American Conservative Thought* (New York: Harper & Row, 1988), pp. 21, 29, 38.
67. *Time Magazine*. "The Underdog Underdog" (6 November 1964); John Judis, "Barry Goldwater's Curious Campaign," (Alicia Patterson Foundation: http//:aliciapatterson.org/ downloaded July 10, 2013).
68. Barry Goldwater as quoted in *Ibid*.
69. Judis, "Barry Goldwater's Curious Campaign."
70. Dean Burch, as quoted in *Ibid*.
71. Lee Edwards, as reported in Judis, "Barry Goldwater's Curious Campaign."
72. Larson, *A Republican Looks at His Party*.
73. Goldwater, *The Conscience of a Conservative*.
74. Barry Goldwater, "Acceptance Speech," Republican National Convention, 1964.
75. Richardson, *To Make Men Free*, pp.274-275.
76. Barry Goldwater, *With No Apologies: The Personal and Political Memoirs of United States Senator Barry M. Goldwater* (New York: William Morrow and Co., 1979); John Dean, *Broken Government: How Republican Rule Destroyed the Legislative, Executive, and Judicial Branches* (New York: Penguin, 2007).
77. Barry Goldwater, "Acceptance Speech," Republican National Convention, 1964.
78. Goldwater, *With No Apologies*.
79. Barry Goldwater, Speech in the U.S. Senate (September 16, 1981).
80. Barry Goldwater (November 1994), as quoted in John W. Dean, *Conservatives Without Conscience* (New York: Penguin, 2006).
81. Barry Goldwater, as quoted in Lloyd Grove, "Barry Goldwater's Left Turn," *Washington Post* (28 July, 1994).
82. Curtis White, *The Science Delusion: Asking the Big Questions in a Culture of Easy Answers* (Brooklyn, N.Y.: Melville House, 2013).
83. Daniel Lazare, *The Frozen Republic: How the Constitution Is Paralyzing Democracy* (New York: Harcourt Brace & Co., 1996).

84. Martin Heidegger, "The Question Concerning Technology" in Martin Heidegger, *The Question Concerning Technology and Other Essays*, Trans. William Lovitt (New York: Harper & Row, 1977).
85. *Ibid.*
86. Arendt, *The Human Condition*; Carl Schmitt, *The Concept of the Political*, Trans. George Schwab (Chicago: Univ. of Chicago Press, 1996); Allan Bloom, *The Closing of the American Mind* (New York: Simon and Schuster, 1987).
87. *Ibid.*; Oakeshott, "Rationalism in Politics"; Arendt, *The Human Condition*; Arendt, *The Promise of Politics*; Aristotle, *Politics*.
88. Aristotle, *Nicomachean Ethics*. Trans. Robert C. Bartlett and Susan D. Collins (Chicago: Univ. of Chicago Press, 2012).
89. Aristotle, *Politics*; Schmitt, *The Concept of the Political*.
90. Donald Phillip Verene, *Philosophy and the Return to Self-Knowledge* (New Haven: Yale Univ. Press, 1971); Giambattista Vico, *The New Science of Giambattista Vico* 3rd ed. (1744), trans. Thomas Goddard Bergin and Max Harold Fisch (Ithaca: Cornell University Press).
91. Francis Fukuyama, "The End of History?" *The National Interest* 16 (Summer 1989): 3-18.
92. Fukuyama, *The End of History and the Last Man*; Hegel *Phenomenology of Spirit*; Alexandre Kojeve, *Introduction to the Reading of Hegel: Lectures on the Phenomenology of Spirit*, ed. Allan Bloom, Trans. James H. Nichols Jr. (Ithaca: Cornell Univ. Press, 1980).
93. Victor Gourevitch, "The End of History?" *Interpretation* 21:2 (Winter 1993-1994) *passim*, p.215.
94. *Ibid.*; Immanuel Kant, "Perpetual Peace: A Philosophic Sketch," in *Kant's Political Writings*, ed. Hans Reiss. Trans. H. B. Nisbet (Cambridge: Cambridge Univ. Press, 1970; 2nd enlarged ed. 1991).
95. Gourevitch, "The End of History?," p.221.
96. Fukuyama, *The End of History and the Last Man*.
97. Immanuel Kant, "On the Common Saying: 'This May be True in Theory, but it does not Apply in Practice'," in *Kant's Political Writings*, ed. Hans Reiss. Trans. H. B. Nisbet (Cambridge: Cambridge Univ. Press, 1970; 2nd enlarged ed. 1991).

98. Plato, *The Republic of Plato*. Ed. & Trans. Allan Bloom (New York: Basic Books, 1991).
99. Aristotle, *Politics*; Leo Strauss, "On Tyranny" and "Restatement on Xenophon's Hiero," in Leo Strauss *On Tyranny* rev. ed., ed. Victor Gourevitch and Michael S. Roth (Chicago: Univ. of Chicago Press, 2000).
100. Gourevitch, "The End of History?"; Strauss, "On Tyranny"; Aristotle, *Politics*.
101. Oakeshott, "Rationalism in Politics."
102. Fukuyama, *The End of History and the Last Man*, especially see the later chapters regarding this problem.
103. Strauss, "On Tyranny"; Strauss, "Restatement on Xenophon's Hiero"; Schmitt, *On the Concept of the Political*; Friedrich Nietzsche, "The Greek State" in Friedrich Nietzsche, *On the Genealogy of Morality* rev. Student Ed., Trans. Carol Diethe. Ed. Keith Ansell Pearson (Cambridge: Cambridge Univ. Press, 2007).
104. Vico, *New Science*; Friedrich Nietzsche, *The Advantages and Disadvantages of History for Life*. Trans. Peter Preuss (Indianapolis: Hackett, 1980).
105. Aristotle, *Politics*; Aristotle, *Nicomachean Ethics*.
106. Schmitt, *The Concept of the Political*; Arendt *The Human Condition*.
107. Plato, *The Republic of Plato*.
108. Schmitt, *The Concept of the Political*; Arendt *The Human Condition*.
109. Gourevitch, "The End of History?," p.217.
110. George Grant, *Technology and Empire* (Toronto: House Of Anansi, 1991); Rahe, *Soft Despotism*.
111. Hannah Arendt, *The Origins of Totalitarianism* (New York: Meridian, 1958); David K. Shipler, *The Rights of the People: how Our Search for Safety Invades Our Liberties* (New York: Alfred A. Knopf, 2011).
112. John Rawls, *Justice as Fairness: A Restatement*, ed. Erin Kelly (Cambridge: Harvard Univ. Press, 1981); Michael J. Sandel, "The Procedural Republic and the Unencumbered Self," *Political Theory* 12:1 (Fall 1984): 81-96.

113. Arendt, *Origins of Totalitarianism*. Note the Arendt begins to formulate an explanation of totalitarian violence as an early stage of totalitarianism, with implications that violence signals an incomplete totalitarianism, with violence replacing conviction and commitment to the state and government. This implies that a successful and mature totalitarian movement and state would not have violence, but would have ideological commitment in its place with no need of violence to enforce adherence to the system and its ideals.

114. Rahe, *Soft Despotism*, Alexandre Kojeve, "Tyranny and Wisdom," in Leo Strauss *On Tyranny* rev. ed., ed. Victor Gourevitch and Michael S. Roth (Chicago: Univ. of Chicago Press, 2000).

115. *Ibid.*

116. Rahe, *Soft Despotism*; Kojeve, "Tyranny and Wisdom"; Fukuyama, *The End of History and the Last Man*.

117. Schmitt, *On the Concept of the Political*.

118. Tocqueville, *Democracy in America* vol.2; Schmitt, *On the Concept of the Political*; John Marini, "Bureaucracy and America: Leo Strauss on Constitutionalism, the State, and Tyranny," in Kenneth L. Deutsch and John A. Murley, eds. *Leo Strauss, the Straussians, and the American Regime* (Rowman & Littlefield, 1999).

119. Strauss, "On Tyranny"; Strauss, "Restatement on Xenophon's Hiero"; Schmitt, *On the Concept of the Political*.

120. Rahe, *Soft Despotism, passim*; see Georges Bataille, "The Psychological Structure of Fascism," in Georges Bataille, *Visions of Excess: Selected Writings 1927-1939*, (Theory and History of Literature Vol.14). Ed. Allan Stoekl (Minneapolis: Univ. of Minnesota Press, 1985), which makes this argument by implication despite its being the opposite of the author's Marxist intentions and desire/prediction.

121. Fukuyama, *The End of History and the Last Man*; for more challenging philosophic and original versions of this theory and its accompanying ideas see Kojeve, *Introduction to the Reading of Hegel* and Hegel, *Phenomenology of Spirit*.

122. Fukuyama, "The End of History?"

123. Alfred S. Regnery, "The Pillars of Modern American Conservatism," in *The Intercollegiate Review* (Spring 2012).
124. Fukuyama, "The End of History?"; Fukuyama, *The End of History and the Last Man.*
125. Regnery, "The Pillars of Modern American Conservatism."
126. *Ibid.*
127. *Ibid.*
128. Frank, *What's the Matter with Kansas*, pp.6-10.
129. Burke, *Reflections on the Revolution in France.*
130. Richardson, *To Make Men Free*, pp.290-291.
131. Saloma III, *Ominous Politics*, pp.98-99; Richardson, *To Make Men Free*, pp.276-280.
132. *Ibid.*, p.291; Wills, *Reagan's America*, p.455.
133. Matthew Yglesias, "Why Did The South Turn Republican?" in *The Atlantic Monthly* (August 24, 2007) http://www.theatlantic.com/politics/archive/2007/08/why-did-the south-turn-republican/45956/
134. Richardson, *To Make Men Free*, pp.286-290.
135. *Ibid.*, pp.289-290.
136. David Shribman, "Washington Talk; Neoconservatives and Reagan: Uneasy Coalition" in *The New York Times* (September 28, 1981). http://www.nytimes.com/1981/09/28/us/washington-talk-neoconservatives-and-reagan uneasy-coalition.html?pagewanted=all
137. *Ibid.*
138. Richardson, *To Make Men Free*, pp.290-292.
139. Goldberg, *Liberal Fascism*, p.391.
140. Richard Weaver 1962, as quoted in Goldberg, *Liberal Fascism*, p.391; Goldberg, *Liberal Fascism* pp.391-392.
141. *Ibid.*, p.393.
142. *Ibid.*, p.394.
143. *Ibid.*, p.394.
144. Saloma III, *Ominous Politics*, pp.7-49.
145. *Ibid.*, p.14.

146. *Ibid.*, pp.14-16.
147. *Ibid.*, pp.15-16.
148. *Ibid.*, pp.15-16.
149. Garry Wills, as quoted in Frank, *What's the Matter with Kansas?* p.144.
150. Saloma III, *Ominous Politics*, pp.7-49.
151. Bruce Bartlett, "Why Ronald Reagan Would Not Lead Today's GOP" in *The Fiscal Times* (June 15, 2012) http://www.thefiscaltimes.com/Columns/2012/06/15/Why-Ronald Reagan-Would-Not-Lead-Todays-GOP.
152. Peter Dale Scott, *The Road to 911,* University of California Press, Copyright 2007. pp. 97.
153. Lynn Rosellini, "Health Post Choice Withdraws Amid Controversy," *The New York Times (*April 26, 1981).
154. Saloma III, *Ominous Politics, The New Conservative Labyrinth* (1984), Hill and Wang Publ., New York.
155. Ronald Reagan, "First Inaugural Address (1981)," in Kenneth M. Dolbeare and Michael S. Cummings eds., *American Political Thought*, 6 th ed. (Washington, D. C.: Congressional Quarterly Press, 2010), pp.541-544.
156. *Ibid.*
157. Fukuyama, *The End of History and the Last Man.*
158. Arendt, *The Human Condition.*
159. Desmond S. King, *The New Right: Politics, Markets and Citizenship* (Chicago: The Dorsey Press, 1987), p.139; Garry Wills, *Head and Heart: American Christianities* (New York: Penguin, 2007), pp.491-492.
160. Frank, *What's the Matter with Kansas*, p. 7.
161. Chester E. Finn, "Affirmative Action" in *Commentary* (April 1, 1982) https://www.commentarymagazine.com/articles/affirmative-action-under-reagan/.
162. Wills, *Head and Heart*, pp.490-491.
163. *Ibid.*, pp.491-492.
164. *Ibid.*, p.492.
165. Rory Carroll, "The myth of Ronald Reagan: pragmatic moderate or radical conservative?" in *The Guardian* (September 19, 2015) http://www.

theguardian.com/us news/2015/sep/19/political-myth-ronald-reagan-epublican-moderate-conservative.

166. Chris Good, "On Social Issues, Tea Partiers Are Not Libertarians," in *The Atlantic* (October 6, 2010) http://www.theatlantic.com/politics/archive/2010/10/on-social-issues-tea partiers-are-not-libertarians/64169/.

167. Jeffery Bell, "Social Issues Bring in the Popular Vote for Republicans," in *U.S News and World Report*, (February 28, 2012) http://www.usnews.com/debate-club/will-the-culture wars-benefit-the-gop-in-the-2012-election/social-issues-bring-in-the-popular-vote-for republicans.

168. Frank, *What's the Matter with Kansas*, p.6.

169. Richardson, *To Make Men Free*, p.296.

170. *Ibid.*, p.296.

171. Richardson, *To Make Men Free*, p.293.

172. *Ibid.*, p.293.

173. Raymond Bauer, "The Bolshevik Attitude Toward Science," in Carl Friedrich ed., *Totalitarianism* (New York: Grosset & Dunlap, 1954), pp.141-156.

174. Haynes Johnson, "Devilishly Clever," in *The Washington Post* (January 19, 1990).

175. Haynes Johnson, *Sleepwalking Through History: America in the Reagan Years* (W.W Norton and Company 2003) p.110.

176. Richardson, *To Make Men Free*, p.299.

177. *Ibid.*, p.299.

178. *Ibid.*, p.305.

179. Richardson, *To Make Men Free*, p.305.

180. Richardson, *To Make Men Free*, p.295.

181. Michael Mandelbaum, "Fight Against 'Evil' Communism" in *Council of Foreign Relations* (CFR) (June 8, 2004) http://www.cfr.org/world/fight-against-evil-communism/p7089.

182. Sam Tanenhaus, "Conservatism is Dead" in *The New Republic* (February 17, 2009).

183. *Ibid.*

184. Hannah Arendt, *The Human Condition* (The University of Chicago Press 1998).
185. *Ibid.*, p.33.
186. *Ibid.*
187. Robert E. Kelly, "The National Debt: From FDR (1941) to Clinton (1996) (McFarland and Company, Inc., Publishers 2000) p.174.
188. NPR Staff, "Ike's Warning of Military Expansion, 50 Years Later," in NPR (January 17, 2011) http://www.npr.org/2011/01/17/132942244/ikes-warning-of-military-expansion 50-years-later.
189. Clifford Owen and Nathan Tarcov, *The Legacy of Rousseau* (The University of Chicago Press 1997) p.148.
190. Will Bunch, "Five myths about Ronald Reagan's Legacy," in *The Washington Post* (February 4, 2011) https://www.washingtonpost.com/opinions/five-myths-about-ronald reagans-legacy/2011/02/04/ABs1qxQ_story.html.
191. Paul Krugman, "Debunking the Regan Myth" in *The New York Times* (January 21, 2008) http://www.nytimes.com/2008/01/21/opinion/21krugman.html?_r=0.
192. Harvey C. Mansfield, *America's Constitutional Soul* (The Johns Hopkins Univ. Press, 1993).
193. Richardson, *To Make Men Free*, pp.311-312.
194. Wills, *Head and Heart*, pp.492-493.
195. *Ibid.*, p.308.
196. Wills, *Head and Heart*, pp.492-493.
197. Stephen Skowronek, *The Politics Presidents Make: Leadership from John Adams to George Bush* (Cambridge: Belknap Press, 1993).
198. *Ibid.*
199. Richardson, *To Make Men Free*, p.310.
200. *Ibid.*, p.313.
201. *Ibid.*, pp.312-319.
202. *Ibid.*, p.310.
203. *Ibid.*, p.310.

204. Frank, *What's the Matter With Kansas?* p.13.
205. Richardson, *To Make Men Free*, p.310.
206. *Ibid.*, p.310.
207. Blumenthal, *Republican Gomorrah*, p.87.
208. E. J. Dionne Jr., *Our Divided Political Heart: The Battle for the American Idea in an Age of Discontent* (New York: Bloomsbury, 2012).
209. *Ibid.*
210. *Ibid.*
211. Newt Gingrich, *To Renew America* (New York: HarperCollins, 1995), pp.34-35.
212. Blumenthal, *Republican Gomorrah*, p.88.
213. *Ibid.*, p.88.
214. *Ibid.*, p.88.
215. *Ibid.*, p.91.
216. Gingrich, *Lessons Learned the Hard Way: A Personal Report* (New York: HarperCollins, 1998), p.168.
217. *Ibid.*, p.168.
218. *Ibid.*, p.169.
219. *Ibid.*, p.176.
220. *Ibid.*, p.173.
221. *Ibid.*, p.165; note that Gingrich uses "movement" and "activists" throughout this book while describing his "conservatism" and "conservatives."
222. *Ibid.*, p.165.
223. *Ibid.*, pp.166-167.
224. *Ibid.*, p.167.
225. *Ibid.*, p.167.
226. *Ibid.*, p.168.
227. *Ibid.*, p.168.
228. *Ibid.*, p.173.
229. *Ibid.*, pp.173-176; Sheryl Gay Stolberg, "Swing-State Governor Could Enliven a Crowded Republican Field: Kasich of Ohio Considers Path to Nomination," *New York Times* (March 20, 2015).

230. Newt Gingrich, *To Renew America* (New York: HarperCollins, 1995), p.190.
231. *Ibid.*, p.189.
232. Gingrich, *Lessons Learned the Hard Way*, p.179.
233. *Ibid.*, p.179.
234. *Ibid.*, pp.82-83.
235. Gingrich, *To Renew America*, p.36.
236. *Ibid.*, pp.29-34.
237. *Ibid.*, p.10.
238. *Ibid.*, p.80.
239. *Ibid.*, pp.63-69.
240. *Ibid.*, p.74.
241. *Ibid.*, pp.74-84.
242. *Ibid.*, pp.74-84.
243. Gingrich, *Lessons Learned the Hard Way*, p.170.
244. *Ibid.*, p.170.
245. *Ibid.*, pp.165-171.
246. Will, *The Woven Figure*, p.85.
247. Will, *The Woven Figure*, p.247.
248. Gingrich, *Lessons Learned the Hard Way*, p.80 and throughout.
249. *Ibid.*, p.106.
250. Richardson, *To Make Men Free*, p.313.
251. *Ibid.*, pp.313-314.
252. Ed Gillespie, and Bob Schellhas, eds. *Contract with America: The Bold Plan by Rep. Newt Gingrich, Rep. Dick Armey and the House Republicans to Change the Nation* (New York: Random House, 1994).
253. *Ibid.*, p.6.
254. John Locke, *Second Treatise of Government*, Ed. C. B. Macpherson (Indianapolis: Hackett, 1980).
255. Gillespie and Schellhas, *Contract with America*, p.6.
256. *Ibid.*, p.4.
257. *Ibid.*, pp.9-10.
258. Will, *The Woven Figure*, p.85.

259. Gillespie and Schellhas, *Contract with America*, p.5.
260. *Ibid.*, p.5.
261. *Ibid.*, p.6, 13.
262. *Ibid.*, p.13.
263. *Ibid.*, p.12.
264. *Ibid., p.15.*
265. *Ibid.*, p.16.
266. *Ibid.*, pp.45-46.
267. *Ibid.*, p.46.
268. *Ibid.*, pp.43-44.
269. *Ibid.*, p.21.
270. *Ibid.*, pp.126-131, 143-155.
271. Goldberg, *Liberal Fascism*, p.400.
272. Richardson, *To Make Men Free*, p.316.
273. Blumenthal, *Republican Gomorrah*, p.85.
274. *Ibid.*, p.84.
275. *Ibid.*, p.85.
276. *Ibid.*, p.85.
277. *Ibid.*, p.85.
278. *Ibid.*, p.85.
279. *Ibid.*, p.85.
280. *Ibid.*, pp.85-86.
281. *Ibid.*, p.86.
282. *Ibid.*, p.86.
283. *Ibid.*, p.87.
284. *Ibid.*, p.87.
285. Tom Delay, as quoted in Blumenthal, *Republican Gomorrah*, p.87.
286. Gingrich, *Lessons Learned the Hard Way*, pp.149-154.
287. *Ibid.*, p.154.
288. *Ibid.*, pp.149, 150, 152, 153, 154, 157.
289. *Ibid.*, p.158.
290. *Ibid.*, p.159.
291. Blumenthal, *Republican Gomorrah*, p.89.

292. *Ibid.*, p.89.
293. *Ibid.*, pp.89-91.
294. *Ibid.*, p.89.
295. *Ibid.*, pp.89-90.
296. *Ibid.*, p.91; Richardson, *To Make Men Free*, p.321.
297. *Ibid.*, pp.321-322.
298. Blumenthal, *Republican Gomorrah*, p.91.
299. *Ibid.*, p.97.
300. *Ibid.*, p.97.
301. *Ibid.*, p.97.
302. *Ibid.*, p.98.
303. *Ibid.*, pp.99-100.
304. Blumenthal, *Republican Gomorrah*, pp.10, 97; Dean, *Conservatives Without Conscience*, pp.118-132.
305. *Ibid.*, pp.127-128.
306. *Ibid.*, pp.137-138; Blumenthal, *Republican Gomorrah*, pp.100-101.
307. *Ibid.*, p.115; Dean, *Conservatives Without Conscience*, pp.132-137.
308. Blumenthal, *Republican Gomorrah*, pp.101.
309. *Ibid.*, p.101.
310. *Ibid.*, pp.101-102.
311. *Ibid.*, pp.101-102.
312. *Ibid.*, p.102.
313. *Ibid.*, p.102.
314. *Ibid.*, p.102.
315. *Ibid.*, p.102.
316. *Ibid.*, p.102-106.
317. *Ibid.*, 102
318. *Ibid.*, p.104.
319. *Ibid.*, p.105.
320. *Ibid.*, pp.103-109, 113.
321. *Ibid.*, p.113.
322. *Ibid.*, p.114.
323. *Ibid.*, p.115.

324. *Ibid.*, p.115.
325. *Ibid.*, p.116.
326. *Ibid.*, p.116.
327. *Ibid.*, p.116.
328, pp.116-117.. *Ibid.*, p.116.
329. *Ibid.*, p.117.
330. *Ibid.*, p.117.
331. *Ibid.*, p.118.
332. Clarke E. Cochrane, *et al.*, *American Public Policy: An Introduction* (New York: St. Martin's Press, 1993).
333. Chris Bates, *Understanding The Federalist to Better Understand the Constitution: Does Publius's 'Split Personality' Pose a Problem?* Honors Thesis (Provo, UT: Brigham Young University, 2007).
334. *Ibid.*
335. *Ibid.*
336. *Ibid.*
337. Blumenthal, *Republican Gomorrah*, pp.117-119.
338. *Ibid.*, p.122.
339. *Ibid.*, pp.122-123.
340. *Ibid.*, pp.123-124.
341. *Ibid.*, pp.122-124.
342. *Ibid*, pp.94-95.
343. Gillespie and Schellhas, *Contract With America*, pp.181-196.
344. *Ibid.*, p.182.
345. *Ibid.*, p.185.
346. *Ibid.*, p.186.
347. Gingrich, *To Renew America*, pp.3-7, 217-222.
348. *Ibid.*, p.6.
349. *Ibid.*, pp.37-40.
350. *Ibid.*, p.7.
351. *Ibid.*, pp.32-33.
352. Richard Rorty, *Achieving Our Country: Leftist Thought in Twentieth-Century America* (Cambridge: Harvard Univ. Press, 1998).

353. Gingrich, *To Renew America*, p.33.
354. *Ibid.*, p.34.
355. *Ibid.*, p.34.
356. *Ibid.*, p.153.
357. OPB Frontline, Introduction, February 20, 2003, http://www.pbs.org/wgbh/pages/frontline/shows/iraq/etc/synopsis.html.
358. *Ibid.*
359. Max Boot and Jeane J. Kirkpatrick, "Think Again: Neocons," *Council on Foreign Relations*, January/ February 2004, http://www.cfr.org/united-states/think-again neocons/p7592.
360. Julian Borger, "The brains," *The Guardian*, March 8, 2004, http://www.theguardian.com/world/2004/mar/09/uselections2004.usa1.
361. Fred Barnes, "Beyond Rove," *The Weekly Standard*, August 13, 2007, http://www.weeklystandard.com/beyond-rove/article/15098.
362. Doug Bandow, "Liberals Are Dressing Up In Conservative Clothes," *CATO Institute*, October 13, 1997, http://www.cato.org/publications/commentary/liberals-are-dressing conservative-clothes.
363. George W. Bush Jr., "THE REPUBLICANS; Bush Outlines His Goals: 'I Want to Change the Tone of Washington,'" *The New York Times,* August 4, 2000, http://www.nytimes.com/2000/08/04/us/the-republicans-bush-outlines-his-goals-i-want to-change-the-tone-of-washington.html?pagewanted=all.
364. Jacob Heilbrunn, "The Shadow President" *The New York Times*, October 12, 2008, http://query.nytimes.com/gst/fullpage.html?res=9C04E4D71F39F931A25753C1A6E9C8B63&pagewanted=all.
365. *Ibid.*
366. Simon Maxwell Apter, "Bush, Cheney In History's First Drafts," *NPR*, October 2008, http://www.npr.org/templates/story/story.php?storyId=95335622.
367. Jake Tapper, "I pick me!" *Salon*, http://www.salon.com/2000/07/26/nominee/.
368. *The World According to Dick Cheney*, directed by R.J. Cutler (2012; Showtime Network, 2013), DVD.
369. William Rusher, "Should Bush Keep Cheney?" *Cherokee County Herald*, August 18, 2004.

370. Christopher D. O'Sullivan, "Marginalizing Colin Powell Was a Huge Mistake," *The New York Times,* September 17, 2013, http://www.nytimes.com/roomfordebate/2013/09/16/foggy-bottom-and-the-fog-of war/marginalizing-colin-powell-was-a-huge-mistake.

371. Oliver Burkeman, "Rumsfeld's progress," *The Guardian,* November 9, 2006, http://www.theguardian.com/world/2006/nov/10/midterms2006.iraq1.

372. Sidney Blumenthal, "The Long March of Dick Cheney," *The Washington Post,* November 27, 2005, http://historynewsnetwork.org/article/18668.

373. John Nichols, "Searching for the Praetorian Guard at the George W. Bush Museum," *The Nation,* April 25, 2013, http://www.thenation.com/article/searching-praetorian-guard george-w-bush-museum/.

374. Bcgnt, "Cheney 1994 Argues Against Going Into Baghdad. Bush Said, "Bring It On!" *Daily KOS,"* August 16, 2007, http://www.dailykos.com/story/2007/8/16/372245/-.

375. R.J. Cutler, *The World According to Dick Cheney.*

376. *Ibid.*

377. Steven L. Danver, *Encyclopedia of Politics of the American West,* (CQ Press: 2013), p. 585.

378. Karen Tumulty and James Carney, "Bush's Fuzzy Science," *Time,* September 10, 2001, p.35.

379. Peter Beinhart, *The Icarus Syndrome,* (New York: HarperCollins Publishers, 2010), p.326.

380. Marc J. Ambinder, "Inside the Council for National Policy," *ABC News,* May 2, 2002, http://abcnews.go.com/Politics/story?id=121170&page=1.

381. George W. Bush, "Address by George W. Bush, 2001," Joint Congressional Committee on Inaugural Ceremonies," January 2001, http://www.inaugural.senate.gov/swearing- in/address/address-by-george-w-bush-2001.

382. OPB Frontline, "New Rules," 2002, http://www.pbs.org/wgbh/pages/frontline/shows/schools/nochild/nclb.html.

383. Martin R. West, "No Child Left Behind: How to Give It a Passing Grade," *Brookings,* December 2005, http://www.brookings.edu/research/papers/2005/12/education-west.
384. Associated Press, "States Rebelling Against No Child Left Behind," February 17, 2004, http://www.foxnews.com/story/2004/02/17/states-rebelling-against-no-child-left-behind.html.
385. Emmanuel Touhey, "Education secretary: 'No Child Left Behind' has led to a 'dumbing down,'" *The Hill,* January 28, 2011, http://thehill.com/blogs/congress-blog/the administration/140977-interview-with-education-secretary-arne-duncan.
386. Charles R. Kessler and John B. Kienker, *Life, Liberty and The Pursuit of Happiness: Ten Years of The Claremont Review of Books,* (Maryland: Rowman and Littlefield Publishers), p. 26.
387. Michael S. Northcott, *Angel Directs the Storm: Apocalyptic Religion and American Empire,* (New York: I.B Tauris), p.41.
388. WNYC, "The Patriot Act's Unintended Consequences," WNYC, May 29, 2015, http://www.wnyc.org/story/patriot-acts-unintended-consequences/.
389. Faiz Shakir, Amanda Terkel, Satyam Khanna, Matt Corley, Benjamin Armbruster, Ali Frick, and Ryan Powers, "Introducing PNAC 2.0," *The Huffington Post,* May 25, 2011, http://www.huffingtonpost.com/the-progress-report/introducing-pnac-20_b_181307.html.
390. Ron Suskind, "Faith, Certainty and the Presidency of George W. Bush," *The New York Times Magazine,* October 17. 2004, http://www.nytimes.com/2004/10/17/magazine/faith certainty-and-the-presidency-of-george-w-bush.html?_r=0.
391. R.J. Cutler, *The World According to Dick Cheney.*
392. Earl H. Fry, *Lament for America: Decline of the Superpower, Plan for Renewal* (Canada: University of Toronto Press, 2010), p.82.
393. Peter D. Feaver, "Cold War II," *The Weekly Standard,* October 1, 2011, http://www.weeklystandard.com/cold-war-ii/article/1418.

394. Jonah Goldberg, "Liberal Fascism: The Secret History of the American Left, From Mussolini to the Politics of Meaning," (New York: Doubleday, 2008), p. 401.
395. Chris Hedges, *American Fascists: The Christian Right and the War on the America*, (New York: Free Press, 2006) p.23.
396. *Ibid.*
397. ABC News, "Falwell Apologizes for Placing Blame," *ABC,* September 20, 2001, http://abcnews.go.com/GMA/story?id=126698&page=1.
398. R.J. Cutler, *The World According to Dick Cheney.*
399. Susan K. Harris, *Gods Arbiters: Americans and the Philippines, 1898 – 1902* (New York: Oxford University Press, 2011), p. 14.
400. Earl H. Fry, *Lament for America: Decline of the Superpower,* p. 21.
401. Jaron Lanier, *Who Owns the Future?* (New York: Simon and Schuster, 2013) p. 208.
402. Earl H. Fry, *Lament for America: Decline of the Superpower,* p. 19.
403. Earl H. Fry, *Lament for America: Decline of the Superpower,* p. 69.
404. Ronald Wright, *What is America? A Short History of The New World Order,* (Toronto: Da Capo Press, 2008), p.221.
405. Lauren Fox, "Freshman Republicans in Congress Here to Stay," *U.S. News and World Report,* July 7, 2012, http://www.usnews.com/news/articles/2012/07/07/freshman republicans-in-congress-here-to-stay.
406. Norman J. Orenstein and Thomas E. Mann, "Five Delusions About Our Broken Politics," *The American Interest,* June 10, 2012, http://www.the-american interest.com/2012/06/10/five-delusions-about-our-broken-politics/.
407. Michael Gerson, "Why the Tea Party Is Toxic for the GOP," *Washington Post,* August 25, 2010.
408. Frank Newport, "Tea Party Support Holds at 24%," *Gallup,* October 1, 2014, accessed January 5, 2015, http://www.gallup.com/poll/177788/tea-party-support-holds.aspx.
409. *Ibid.*
410. *Ibid.*

411. "Analysis: Obama pitches middle while GOP eyes base," *The Associated Press*, February 2012, accessed December 7, 2014, http://nbcpolitics.nbcnews.com/_news/2012/02/12/10389107-analysis-obama-pitches middle-while-gop-eyes-base.

412. Ryan Hecker, "Contract from America," September 1, 2010, accessed December 5, 2013, http://contractfromamerica.org/tag/ryan-hecker/.

413. Lydia Saad, "Voters, Especially Independents, Lack Interest in Election," *Gallup Poll,* November 2014, accessed January 7, 2015, http://www.gallup.com/poll/179147/voters especially-independents-lack-interest-election.aspx.

414. Sara Jarman, "As independent voters increase, emergence of a viable third party looms," *KSL.com,* December 3, 2014, accessed January 5, 2015, http://www.ksl.com/?nid=757&sid=32600639.

415. Samara Klar and Yanna Krupnikov, "Independents didn't decide the midterm election," *The Washington Post*, November 6, 2014, accessed December 5, 2014, http://www.washingtonpost.com/blogs/monkey-cage/wp/2014/11/06/independents-didnt decide-the-midterm-election/.

416. Charlie Crist and Ellis Henican, *The Party's Over: How the Extreme Right Hijacked the GOP and I Became a Democrat* (New York: Dutton, 2014).

417. *Ibid.*

418. *Ibid.*

419. Scott Goodson, "Why Brand Building Is Important," *Forbes,* May 27, 2012, accessed February 12, 2013, http://www.forbes.com/sites/marketshare/2012/05/27/why-brand building-is-important/.

420. "21.5% Youth Turnout: Two-Day Estimate Comparable to Recent Midterm Years," *CIRCLE* (The Center for Information and Research on Civic Learning and Engagement), November 5, 2014, accessed November 16, 2014, http://www.civicyouth.org/21-3-youth-turnout-preliminary-estimate-comparable to-recent-midterm-years/.

421. Sara Jarman, "#rebrand," *The Hill,* October 11, 2013, accessed on December 5, 2013, http://thehill.com/blogs/congress-blog/politics/327829-rebrand.

422. Joshua Green, "Jim DeMint, Congressional Republicans' Shadow Speaker," *Bloomberg Business Week*, September 26, 2013, accessed November 14, 2013, http://www.bloomberg.com/bw/authors/2956-joshua-green.

423. Public Papers of the Presidents of the United Sates: George W. Bush: Book I- January to June 20, 2008. (United States Government Printing Office: 2012).

424. Sara Jarman, "As independent voters increase, emergence of a viable third party looms," *KSL.com,* December 3, 2014, accessed January 5, 2015, http://www.ksl.com/?nid=757&sid=32600639.

425. Zeke J Miller, "All The President's Celebrities: How The White House Used Stars To Sell Obamacare," *TIME,* April 1, 2014, accessed May 5, 2014, http://time.com/45613/obamacare-celerbrities-7-million-ellen-degeneres/.

426. Lisa Mascaro, "Republicans wrestle with dissent on budget cuts," The Los Angeles Times, January 24, 2011, accessed December 5, 2013, http://articles.latimes.com/2011/jan/24/nation/la-na-gop-budget-20110125.

427. Mike Lee, "A New Agenda," *National Review* 65: 22, November 25, 2013, 33-35.

428. *Ibid.*

429. Paul J. Saunders, "The GOP's Identity Crisis," *The National Interest* 130, March/April 2014, 9-19.

430. *Ibid.*

431. Tucker Carlson, "Donald Trump Is Shocking, Vulgar and Right," POLITICO, http://www.politico.com/magazine/story/2016/01/donald-trump-is-shocking-vulgar-and right-213572, January 28, 2016, accessed February 7, 2016.

432. Jacob Heilbrunn, "Springtime for Neocons," *The National Interest* 134, November/December 2014, 5-10.

433. R. J. Cutler, *The World According to Dick Cheney* (Showtime: DVD, 2013).

434. Glenn Garvin, "Ted Cruz: Loose Cannon or Libertarian Reformer?" *Reason: Free Minds and Free Markets* 49:9 (February 2015): 18-24; Paul

J. Saunders, "The GOP's Identity Crisis," *The National Interest* 130 (March/April 2014): 9-19; Henry Olsen, "The Republican Battlefield," *The National Interest* 130 (March/April 2014): 20-28; Ramesh Ponnuru, "Reform Conservatism: The Republican Party is newly awash with ideas," *National Review* 66:2 (February 24, 2014): 16-19; Jonah Goldberg, "Who's the RINO?" *National Review* 65:22 (November 25, 2013): 10.

435. Ponnuru, "Reform Conservatism," pp.16-19; Ross Douthat, "What is Reform Conservatism?" *New York Times* (May 30, 2013).

436. Sheryl Gay Stolberg, "Swing-State Governor Could Enliven a Crowded Republican Field: Kasich of Ohio Considers Path to Nomination," *New York Times* (March 20, 2015).

437. Newt Gingrich, as quoted in *Ibid*.

438. Stolberg, in *Ibid*.

439. Jerry Austin, as quoted in *Ibid*.

440. Ahmed M. Soliman, "Policies of Polarization," *Empirical Magazine* (February 2013), p.16; James N. Druckman, Erik Peterson, and Rune Slothus, "How Elite Partisan Polarization Affects Public Opinion Formation," *American Political Science Review* 107:1 (February 1013): 57-79.

441. Ahmed M. Soliman, "Policies of Polarization," *Empirical Magazine* (February 2013), p.16; James N. Druckman, Erik Peterson, and Rune Slothus, "How Elite Partisan Polarization Affects Public Opinion Formation," *American Political Science Review* 107:1 (February 1013): 57-79.

442. Slavo Zizek, *Trouble in Paradise: From the End of History to the End of Capitalism* (London: Penguin, 2014), pp.54-55.

443. Michael Smerconish, "Smerconish" (Atlanta: CNN).

444. David Brooks, "The Zero-Sum Moment," *New York Times* (March 20, 2015).

445. Matthew S. Holland, *Bonds of Affection: Civic Charity and the Making of America Winthrop, Jefferson, and Lincoln* (Washington D.C.: Georgetown Univ. Press, 2007).

446. *Ibid.*, pp.21-90.
447. *Ibid.*, pp.40, 58-59.
448. *Ibid.*, pp.27-90; "John Winthrop's A Model of Christian Charity Speech," in *Ibid.* pp.261 276.
449. Holland, *Bonds of Affection*, pp.93-157.
450. *Ibid.*, pp.132-136.
451. George Grant, *Technology & Empire* (Toronto: Anansi, 1969).
452. Holland, *Bonds of Affection*, pp.128-157.
453. *Ibid.*, pp.161-240.
454. *Ibid.*, pp.219-240.
455. Garry Wills, Lincoln at Gettysburg: The Words that Remade America (New York: Simon & Schuster, 1992).
456. Holland, *Bonds of Affection*, pp.128-157.
457. Jonathan Schell, "A Politics of Natality," *Social Research* 69:2 (Summer 2002), pp.461 471.
458. *Ibid.*, p.461.
459. *Ibid.*, p.461.
460. *Ibid.*, p.467.
461. *Ibid.*, p.468.
462. Aurelian Craiutu, *A Virtue for Courageous Minds: Moderation in French Political Thought, 1748-1830* (Princeton: Princeton Univ. Press, 2012).
463. *Ibid.*, p.238.
464. *Ibid.*, p.239.
465. *Ibid.*, p.239.

Made in the USA
Lexington, KY
11 May 2017